A Histor
Golborne

Previously published as
Gleanings of Golborne History

James E. Bridge

P & D Riley

A History of Golborne

First published as *Gleanings of Golborne History* by the Estate of James Bridge in 1975

This reset and illustrated edition first published 1997 by
P & D Riley (Publishers)
12 Bridgeway East,
Runcorn,
Cheshire WA7 6LD

ISBN: 1 874712 05 0

British Library Cataloguing - in - Publication Data
A Catalogue Record for this book is available from the British Library

Printed in England by Redwood Books, Wiltshire.

Cover picture: Golborne Auxiliary Fire Service (date unknown)

Introduction

GOLBORNE was once described as a market town in the Urban District of Lancashire, situated 189 miles from London by the London, Midland and Scottish Railway, with cotton mills and collieries and a population in 1931 of 7,322.

Since then, of course, things have changed. The mills and collieries have long gone, the railway too disappeared in 1960 under the cuts imposed by the British Government of the time, and the population has increased dramatically. But, equally important to the residents, Golborne is no longer in the traditional county, but is now a small corner of the Borough of Wigan, itself a 'suburb' of Greater Manchester, and not Lancashire.

The soul of its people will always remain Lancastrian though, and visitors should not be surprised to see postal addresses finishing with 'Golborne, Lancs' despite what the mandarins of Whitehall think!

The people of Golborne are a proud people and they have a long and proud history to match, and it is a history which has survived in one form or another for many centuries, and its people have seen the coming of the Romans, Celts, Saxons, Danes and Normans, and numerous other coming and goings by different races and 'tribes'. It has been the centre of activities for all types of trades, from farmers to farriers, from merchants to miners. And though the town has declined in recent years with the closure of many of its traditional industries, the future of Golborne is still assured by the promise of rejuvenation from European budgets. For those who may feel sceptical of the town's future, it is worth bearing in mind that this phase is simply the latest in a long line which has seen Golborne develop into a modern suburban area from its early days.

In the next 100 years it is likely that future historians will be recording still more changes to a landscape which we take for granted today, but which our great-grandchildren will have trouble recognising. That is why it is vital that the people of Golborne respond to change, for change produces future history. And with Golborne the town's history is certain to be recorded into infinity if it refuses to stagnate or simply be absorbed into a wider Metropolitan community.

After all, it would be a sad reflection for Golborne if it regarded itself as merely an appendage of a large district such as Wigan or Greater Manchester after being at the centre of so many activities over the centuries.

Peter Riley

About the Author

After retiring from Park House Farm James Bridge
continued to work with the War Agricultural Committee
and as a magistrate. His leisure time was spent in reading,
painting and writing.
His writings include poems and *Gleanings of Golborne
History*. This was finished shortly before his death in 1955
and was published some years later.

Contents

FOREWORD

For some unknown reason the people who have lived in Golborne do not appear to have thought it necessary to gather together in permanent form particulars of historical interest relating to the township. Mr .G.M. Trevelyan has said that "we cannot understand our present opinions, prejudices and emotional reactions, unless we know what is our history and why it has come down to us." For this reason and because "a place without a history is like a person who has lost his memory," we desire to find out about the people who once lived here; something of their problems and pursuits, their customs, pleasures and opinions. As Bacon remarks: "Out of the monuments, names, proverbs, private records and evidences, fragments of stories, passages of books and the like, we doe save and recorde somewhat of a deluge of time." So these details have been gathered together from stories handed down from one generation to another, from the writings of historians and antiquarians, from old wills, private letters and diaries.

To Mr. T.R. Dootson of Leigh, I am deeply indebted for the placing of his valuable collection of Lancashire Books at my disposal, and for his corrections and personal interest without which I could not have undertaken this task. To several local residents I am also grateful for allowing me the use of documents in their possession. These have been generously placed at my disposal and from them I have quoted freely. *The Victoria History of the County, Lanc. hire History* by Mr Baines, Records of the Lancashire and Cheshire Historical S iety, the Coram Rege Roll 254 relating to South Lancashire in the reign of E ard I, translated by G.H. Tupling, M.A.,Ph.D., have been of great value. These her works have also been used: *Lancashire Inquests* by J.P.Rylands, F.S.A., and r. W. Beamont's version of *The Fee of Makerfield* together with his translation of the parts of Domesday Book which relate to Lancashire and Cheshire. I am indebted to all who have opened up these byways and hope that this work may help others to share my interest in the history of the township and of the surrounding townships with which Golborne is so closely connected. Let Camden's words serve as an introduction to this work:

If there be any who are desirous to be strangers in theire owne soils and
forainers in theire owne citie they may so continue and therein flatter
themselves; for such I have not written these lines nor taken these paines.

7

Acknowledgements

The publishers would like to thank the following for their help:

Mary Bridge, for giving permission to republish her late father's work.

Margaret Holland, for her valuable assistance.

Wigan Archives Department, for use of the photographs in this book.

Chapter 1
Golborne's Past

A geographical and topographical description of the locality later to be known as Golborne places it on the outer edge of the coal measures where, to the North-East, the inhospitable features of an unkindly soil usually associated with coal are perceptible. The pebble beds of the Permian series cover the whole of the township as well as adjoining areas. Numerous faults run from East to West and South to South-East and abundant supplies of water are to be found. There is evidence of red sandstone of a later era in several outcrops. This is to be found in Golborne Hollows and particularly in various disused quarries. It is assumed that the same formation extends from the South-West Lancashire coast to North Cheshire. The area of the township includes approximately 1700 acres and the height above sea level is about 160 feet.

If "history is a matter of rough guessing from all the available facts" those relating to Golborne's early history are comparatively few. We may assume that the area in its primaeval condition was overgrown with bracken, gorse and scrub, or was woodland tract and swamp. Later, a few isolated dwellings were constructed in small clearings which primitive man in his warfare with nature strove to till. The cultivated grain consisted of barley, oats, rye and other coarse grain, together with a mixture known as bere.

A few crude huts thatched with branches of trees, reeds or rushes, with a smoke hole in the roof and crevices for windows served as dwelling places. A charred tree branch or the antlers of deer provided digging utensils, while the tilled plots were no doubt protected against marauding animals by stakes interwoven with branches.

Fishing and hunting were the principal means of subsistence. Nuts, berries, wild honey, certain roots and wild fruit added to the scanty livelihood. For clothing, the skins of animals were used.

Some measure of civilisation came with the Roman occupation. The West of the township contains evidence of this. An old Roman road leading from Warrington by way of Longford, South-West of Winwick Church, by Red Bank, Wargrave, over Crow Lane direct to Lodge Lane, onward to Ashton and the North was discovered some years ago. Remains are not numerous, however, as this part of Britain was less under the influence of Rome than the southern part of the country. After the withdrawal of the Romans this area was affected by the barbarian invasions.

According to the County History "it is believed that a settlement was instituted at Winwick by the Angles." Winwick became the hub of affairs completely overshadowing the smaller settlements of the district. Later, its church was the principal place of worship and the chief burial ground.

In Taylor's *Ancient Crosses of Lancashire* mention is made of "the stone cross of Winwick." The arm of the cross is believed to have been cut over a thousand years ago. The cross, before it was broken, must have been one of the "largest and most remarkable of its kind in England." While some contend that it was a preaching cross of pre-Norman times, others say it was set up as a memorial to St. Oswald in Anglo-Saxon times.

When the Venerable Bede wrote his *Ecclesiastical History* he states that "in the year 634 AD, Oswald came to the throne after the death of his uncle Edwin who had been slain by Penda, and reigned until 642 AD." Oswald's kingdom of Northumbria stretched westward to include this part of Lancashire. When the Christian faith was proclaimed in England, Oswald is said to have been among the first to have received it.

Green in his *Short History of the English People* states that "Oswald in his Youth found refuge in the famous monastery of Iona and, on his accession to the throne, after the death of his uncle, he appealed to the monks of Iona requesting them to send missionaries to preach to the people." This was done but the monks were not very successful. On returning, they stated that success was impossible as the people were both stubborn and barbarous. Aidan, who was among those who listened to their report, asked: "Was it stubbornness, or your severity? Did you forget God's word, to give them milk first and then the meat?" All eyes were turned to the speaker as the fittest to undertake the abandoned mission. So Aidan was sent. "He wandered on foot preaching among the peasants making many converts."

Winwick is said to have been a royal residence of Oswald's. "It was a place dearly loved by him..."
"On one occasion when about to partake of food, poor people came appealing for alms. When this became known to Oswald he caused a silver dish to be broken in pieces and distributed among them so they might provide food for themselves."

Another version of this incident is that Aidan was present when the thegn or noble of the war band whom Oswald had appointed to give alms to the poor at his gate told of a multitude that stood without, fasting. The king at once bade the untasted food to be carried to the poor and his silver dish to be broken and divided piecemeal among them. Aidan seized the royal hand and blessed it. "May this hand" he cried "never grow old."

Legend says that when all else of Oswald had perished the hand that Aidan had blessed "remained white and uncorrupted."

Bede proceeds to mention that the heathen king of Mercia was hostile to the Northumbrians and set out to vanquish Oswald and his supporters. Journeying northward he made a surprise attack on the hastily grouped forces of King Oswald, "at which period he was killed in a great battle at a place called in the English tongue Maserfield, in the thirty-eighth year of his age, on the fifth day of August, 642'. His mutilated body was set on stakes.

Whatever historians say now about the site of the battle, local tradition has it that the place where Oswald is said to have fallen is at the foot of the hill near the Newton-Winwick boundary. It has been the scene of many visitations by historical and other societies. The well, the hermitage, the monk's house, the priory, the ancient cross with its carved figures and the inscription carved in the stone on the south wall of the church, all testify to the memory of Oswald. The inscription reads:

> *'This place of yore did Oswald greatly love,*
> *Northumbria's king but now a saint above*
> *Who in Marcelde's field did fighting fall;*
> *0 blest one hear, when here on Thee we call."*

Regarding Oswald's well Mr.Baines states: "Many took up the very dust of the place and putting it in water did much good with it to those persons who were sick. The custom came so much in use that the earth being carried away by degrees there remained a hole as deep as the height of a man."

Mr. J.E.Worsley, F.S.A., who resided at Winwick, comments: "The earth where Oswald fell, being placed in water is said to have cured many sick people. The earth so taken away caused a hollow in the earth where the water gushed forth from Oswald's well." For many years, before a piped water supply was provided for the residents nearby, Oswald's well was the main source of drinking water.

In *Local Gleanings* (1878) the writer refers to an old man named Roughley who died about 1830. He had been paid three shillings a year to keep Oswald's well clean. A little before 1835 St.Oswald's well was kept free from weed, and water obtained from it was used in certain Catholic chapels.

High Street, Golborne, at the turn of the 20th century.

Some time later the influence of the Danish invaders was also felt in the area. At one time people were obliged to pay the hated Danegeld, but the payments failed to check the settlement of the Danes in the North.

The Hundred

Some three centuries before the Norman Occupation parishes had been formed in England and the country had been divided into Hundreds. Different interpretations have been given to the meaning of this term. It may relate to the area where a hundred families lived or to the division of the county where a hundred men were responsible for the keeping of the peace, or where a similar number were available for military service. It may have been associated with a Saxon law relating to the allotting of land - a tithing granted to ten families with twelve tithings making a Hundred.

Between the Ribble and the Mersey there were six Hundreds and, with slight variation, they remain as originally constituted. These were the Hundreds of Derbie, Walentude, Newton, Salford, Blackburn and Lailand. Within each Hundred were many manors, altogether several hundred in fact between the Mersey and the Ribble.

Some idea may be gathered about the vastness of the Newton Hundred when we realise that Newton, Golborne, Southworth with Croft, Winwick with Hulme, Middleton and Arbury, Woolston with Martinscroft, Poulton with Fearnhead, Ince, Billinge, Pemberton, Orrell, Winstanley, Wigan, Hindley, Abram and Haydock, all of them having manors, were included in it. Local government was administered through the manor courts, the two principal ones being the Court Baron, which dealt with various appointments and the business of the manor, and the Court Leete. If a lord had several manors he might hold Court Leete and deal with criminal cases, as revealed by records translated from Latin and French. Exercising an influence in this district before the Norman Conquest was King Edward the Confessor who is reputed to have had a court at Newton. Other records show that both Court Baron and Court Leete were held at Newton, the last Court Baron being held there in November 1884.

The Domesday Enquiry

From an entry in Domesday Book we learn something of the conditions prevailing here in the late eleventh century. William the Conqueror having consulted with his advisory council - the Witan or King's Council decided to obtain as many particulars as possible about the land, the names of the Principal owners and tenants, the number of hides held by the crown and by freemen together with their value both before the Conquest and at the time of the enquiry. Questions were asked to find out the number of homagers, cotters, freemen, serfs, tenants with hereditary rights, the extent of the woodland, pasture and meadow land, the number of mills, both wind and water driven, and the number of fisheries. The survey commenced in 1085 and was completed in the following year when the reports were put together at Winchester to form what we know as Domesday Book. It is one of the most comprehensive documents ever compiled in our national history. The following translation from the original text is taken from Mr Beamont's book. It supplies interesting details relating to Lancashire and Cheshire.

In Neweton in King; Edward's time there were five hides. Of these, one was in the demesne. The Church of the same manor had one carucate of land free of everything, and St.Oswald of the same vill had two carucates of land free of everything. The other land of this Manor, fifteen men called dreghnes held for fifteen manors which were berewick of the manor, and among them, all of these men rendered thirty shillings.

There is a wood there ten leagues long, and six leagues and two furlongs broad, and there are Hawk aeries. All the free men of this Hundred (except two) as the same custom as the men of West Derbeishire but in August they mowed two days more than they of the King's tillage lands. The two excepted men had five carucates of land, and had forfeitures for bloodshed and rape, and pannage in the woods for their men. The rest were the King's. This manor rendered to the King a farm of Ten pounds and Ten shillings. There are now six Dreghnes and twelve villeins, and four bordars who have nine carucates among them. The demesne is worth four pounds.

The information given in the record is brief, in the king's demesne twenty-two men are recorded, but according to Dr Farrar of the Historical Society the agricultural population would have been about one hundred and twenty persons, total population in Newton being 784. The acreage was 46,000 of which 3,600 acres were arable, exclusive of pasture and waste. The woods of the extensive Hundred covered 88,800 acres.

The Terms Used in Domesday Book

Many of the terms used In the report are now obsolete. The reader may find a brief explanation of some of them helpful.

The Hide: an accepted standard of measurement, generally 120 acres. This unit was computed according to the locality and productivity of the ploughable land or ploughed land. Also, it was estimated to be as much land as would maintain a family for a year. The hide was also called pound land and was rated at 2d. per acre.

Carucate or Car: another term for hide.

Different counties had different standards of measurement. The Lancashire acre contained 7840 sq.yards; the Cheshire acre 10,240 sq.yards. Later, to simplify these existing differences, the imperial or statute acre of 4840 sq.yards was devised.

Virgate: 30 acres of ploughland.,

Bovate: one eighth part of the hide - 15 acres.

When Ethelred imposed his unpopular tax to pay the Danes in 991 AD this tax took the name of Danegeld and the greater part of England including South West Lancashire was subject to it. It was stated at 3d. per bovate.

Oxgang: ten customary acres.

Berewicks: sub-manors.

Panage: the "two excepted men" had "pannage in the woods." This refers to beech mast and acorns which swine were accustomed to eat. According to an ancient law any person found guilty of damaging an oak tree was fined according to the quantity of mast produced by the tree. These two men are presumed to have belonged to Golborne.

Drehgns: comparable with a Norman esquire; an allodial tenant responsible for cultivating the lords land and in addition giving boon service.

Villein: the unfree man; on such men mainly depended the tilling of the land.

Socage: the service of the plough or soc.

Socame: the custom of grinding corn at the communal mill.

Baliwick: the office of Bailiff of the Hundred.

Scutage: tax paid by those who occupied king's land; it was given instead of military service.

Wapentake: division of a shire: a Danish word.

Frankpledge & Tithings: family of ten persons jointly responsible for good conduct.

Pipe Rolls: exchequer rolls, accounts of revenue paid to the crown.

The Newton Hundred of the Middle Ages

At the time of the Domesday Survey, land was an important source of wealth and provided a convenient means of bargaining. After the Conquest, the king deposed many English lords replacing them with Norman barons. Later, he was obliged to reinstate some of the dispossessed English upon conditions of service and allegiance to the crown. These landlords re-let the land on similar terms. All the land between the Ribble and the Mersey was given to Roger of Poictou who had distinguished himself in battle on behalf of his royal master, Roger also had his favourites and he sub-let some of his land in return for knight's service.

The fee of Makerfield (a feudal benefice or gift) Roger allotted to his friend Robert Banastre. This family appears to have had other property in Mellor, Blackburn, Walton-le-Dale, and in Prestatyn, North Wales. Robert Banastre had three sons, Richard, who died in infancy, Warin and Thurstan.

At the time of his father's decease, Warin, not being of age, needed someone to be responsible for monetary payments to the crown. Thomas de Golborne and Adam de Lawton were nominated and they undertook the duty. Warin Banastre married but died leaving no heir so Thurstan, his brother, succeeded to the estates.

Thurstan, as next of kin, is said to have paid a thousand marks to King John to have an Inquest of Office to decide whether the estate of his father and the property of Warin his brother legally belonged to him. The Inquest of Office meant that the sheriff, or other appointee, enquired whether the king's tenant died 'seized of property' of which the reversion accrued to the king. Reliefs or compositions were paid by the lord of the fee on taking up the estate.

Thurstan came into possession and he died in 1218 or 1219 leaving a son named Robert who was one year old at the time. It was this Robert who in later life obtained from the king a charter for markets and fairs in Newton, and fee warren in Newton and Walton-le-Dale. He also founded the chantry in the chapel of Newton anciently called Rokedene, possibly in 1260.

Robert's son, James, married Elena daughter of William de Botiles, or Botler, baron of Warrington. James died in 1293 during his father's lifetime leaving a daughter, Alice, to succeed to the estates.

A slight digression must now be made for we cannot outline Golborne history without describing some of the prevailing conditions in the County Palatine, the turbulent state of society, arrangements relating to marriage and inheritance, forfeiture of lands and other kindred subjects. Returning to Roger of Poictou, the overlord of Robert Banastrre, we may notice how he lost most of his possession for a time. He is said to have committed a treasonable offence and his land was forfeited. Later, he was restored to favour and his land was returned to him during the reign of William Rufus. Evidently past experience profited him little for he became involved in rebellion again and, finally this time, forfeited the land with its valuable manors.

The property passed to Stephen who became king of England. On coming to the throne Stephen gave to his son, William de Blois, the Honor of Lancaster. Later still, Richard I gave it to his brother John of Magna Carta fame.

Edmund Crouchback, the youngest son of Henry III, became Earl of Lancaster and acquired considerable property. He too had a slight connection with the fee of Makerfield.

After his decease, his son Thomas succeeded to the earldoms of Lancaster and Leicester. Thomas on marriage with the heiress of the de Lacy family became possessed of extensive properties in Yorkshire and elsewhere. He was of a quarrelsome disposition and was frequently in trouble. He took a prominent part in the insurrection of the barons which ended in defeat at the Battle of Boroughbridge (1321). He was captured, hastily tried either on the field of battle or at Pontefract without being allowed to defend himself, and was beheaded amid the jeers of the spectators. His property was appropriated for the crown. Parliament, however, was not prepared to accede to the procedure. They criticised the trial, for by a clause in Magna Carta, Thomas should have been judged by his peers. The forfeiture of his estates was held to be legally unsound. So, the decision regarding the estates was rescinded and Henry, his brother and next of kin, succeeded to the title and estates. Later, Lancaster became a County Palatine (a little kingdom within a kingdom) and so remains to this day.

During the Middle Ages with these risings of the barons, crime grew a pace. A state of anarchy prevailed. Groups of partisans fought against each other. Murder, arson and robbery prevailed. Arising out of this turbulent state of affairs were some notable trials held at Wigan in 1323. Golborneites appear to have been mixed up in these troubles for Richard de Lawton of Goldeburne was arrested and indicted at Wigan for "killing Richard le Gappe of Westle (West Leigh) and for sezin and taking away six horses from Newton wood, Oct.2.1323."

Land was considered too important to be left without a man in charge to render service in time of war and pay levies and taxes. A woman in terrorist days was only too glad to have a protector. Widows without children came under feudal rule. The law did not permit an heiress under fourteen years of age, or an heir under twenty, to be without a guardian. When an heiress was under age, the king had a right to choose her a husband. He rarely did so but was content to sell the right to one of his favourites. The guardian took the ward and sometimes married the girl to his son, or married the youth to his daughter. These child-marriages were quite common in the neighbourhood. But there were times when an heiress would revolt and rather than enter into such a marriage was prepared to pay a fine to the crown. Wardship included having custody of the lands and receiving the profits therefrom during the minority of the ward. The custodian was not obliged to render an account of any increment to the ward. By these means many notable families increased their holding of land by hundreds, even thousands, of acres.

Sir John Byrom who was a member of a family with great possessions, land, houses and mills in Golborne, Lowton and surrounding districts, was appointed guardian of the aforementioned Alice Banastre. She was to inherit the fee of Makerfield after the death of her grandfather, Robert Banastre. Sir John had an eye to keeping the properties together for he espoused the heiress to his son. But the marriage was not consummated as the ward was under age. Possibly the girl had spirit enough to object to the alliance. At any rate, Edmund Crouchback, Earl of Lancaster, was appointed guardian in place of Sir John Byrom. Viewed from present day angles the eventual transaction appears mercenary and repulsive. To the earl came the Langtons of West Langton in Leicestershire and "paid a large sum of money to have the custody of Alice Banastre." The earl demanded his price. The Langtons paid it. In due course Alice was married to John Langton. The fee of Makerfield thus passed to the Langton family and was held by them for about three hundred years. Stephen, Archbishop of Canterbury, was perhaps the most distinguished member of the Langton family, and "whatever services he rendered to public order, it was small compared with his service to English freedom," for partly through his agency the power of King John was curtailed by Magna Carta.

The John Langton who married Alice Banastre was knighted by Edward I and obtained from him confirmation of the charter for a market and fee warren in Newton and Walton-le-Dale, and fee warren in Gouldbourne and Lowton. The fee remained in the family until 1604.

In that year, Sir Thomas Langton died at Newton without male issue. The next of kin was Joan Fleetwood, sister to Sir Thomas. Her son, Richard Fleetwood of Caldwich, Stafford, succeeded to the estate. In the first parliament of King James, Sir Richard Fleetwood was mentioned as being the new baron of Newton.

On October 31, 1660, fifty-six years after the death of Sir Thomas Langton, the Fleetwoods sold the manor, borough and barony of Newton with all its messuages and hereditaments to Richard Legh Esq. for £3,500 having previously sold other parts to the same purchaser. William John Legh, reputed twenty-fourth baron in succession to Robert Banastre, was created Lord Newton in 1892.

Some Old Families

An outstanding feature about Golborne is the fact that so many families which were to become famous for various reasons acquired ownership of its land. It is said that long before the Conquest a family of the name Goldeburna resided here and apparently acquired the family name from the name of the place. Later, we hear mention of the following:-

1100 A.D.	Augustine de Golburn in the time of Henry II gave land to William, son of Hamon, who gave to his son Thomas.
1186	Thomas de Golborne paid relief (scutage) on 200 acres.
1200	The name of Parpont or Pierpont appeared.
1212	Thomas de Golborne's demesne consisted of 200 acres. It is also stated that one half of Golborne was held by a family of that name and the other half by the lord of Lowton.
1240 A.D.	Robert Banastre gave to Thurstan de Holland a considerable part of Lowton, namely Byrom Hall. He also had one carucate in Golborne.
1292	Simon, son of Thurstan de Holland, held certain lands in Golborne.
1314	Warin de Golborne gave evidence at an enquiry.
1325	Robert de Golborne gave evidence at an enquiry held at Wigan re Robert de Holland.
1330	Hugh de Haydock's estate consisted of 60 acres in Golborne and other property in the parish of Winwick.
1322	Robert de Holland held several townships in Derbyshire as well as in Lancashire and is shown as holding the Manor of Lightshaw.
1325	Alice, widow of Simon de Holland, claimed dower. We also have the names of Hamon, Levota, Ralph and Thurstan. The descendants of these parties carried the manor of Lightshaw in marriage to Nicholas de Tyldesley. Later, a private act was passed vesting the manor of Golborne-Lightshaw, part of the settled estate of William Duke of Devonshire - in the said Duke and his successors.
1374	Adam de Golborne held a messuage and an oxgang and a half of land. He was outlawed for felony and the land was ceded to the crown.
1403	With the eldest son of Sir Piers Legh of Cheshire- according to Lady Newton in the History of Lyme- their Lancashire connection began. Peter Legh, son of Sir Piers Legh, married Joan, the young daughter

and heiress of Sir Gilbert de Haydock of Haydock. This constituted him in her right lord of Haydock, Poulton, Fearnhead and Bradley. He held these together with other land. The young couple took up residence at Bradley, the ancient seat of the Haydock family. Later, on the field of Agincourt, Peter Legh was knighted. Seven Years afterwards he died in Paris - possibly as a result of the wounds received in the war. His widow married Sir Richard Molyneux of Toxteth and from that connection, it is said, the lords of Sefton originated.

Heath Street, Golborne, early in the 20th century. It is still one of the busiest shopping streets in the town.

Chapter 2
The Origin of Names

The origin of names, either of persons or places, is a subject of great complexity.

How did the name Golborne originate? This is a question which has frequently been asked. Goldeburnam was mentioned as long ago as 969. Records refer to it in 1100; in 1187 the name appears as Goldeburn. In 1314 it was Gold-burn, and it is later mentioned in the Lancashire Pipe Rolls as Golburc, Gowburn and Goldburn.

The word burna relates to a brook, and the word bourne to a boundary. The Millingford Brook is both brook and boundary. The word golde suggests golden or saffron coloured flowers. Most likely marigolds grew along the banks of the burn. This distinguishing feature gave character to the brook - the place where the golden flowers grew - and a name to the settlement which grew up there.

In the past, boundaries of various kinds were often fixed by a ploughed furrow. Later there sprang up a system of enclosures, and crofts, folds, lays, hams and tuns existed in infinite variety.

The tun relates to a tun-ship New-ton, Law-ton. The law is associated with rising ground. Ash-ton is the township of the ash trees. The name Haydock requires more explanation.

The Norman and later English kings were interested in hawking and in the hunting of deer. They exercised strict supervision over the woods, very much to the detriment of the interests of the occupiers of land nearby. Special places were constructed in the forests and woods into which roe deer could be driven. Such enclosures were known as heys. A quick-wood thorn fence, hay or haw-thorn, was mainly used for the purpose (the word quick - quickly growing - is still in use for fences). The planting of oaks was ordered by Edward the Confessor, and according to the philologists the hey and the oak make the place name Hay-d-oak.

The name hey or aye is retained locally to distinguish farm-steads, The Old Hey, The New Hey or Newey for instance and The Heywoods. Also there is the Aye or Hey Brook, another boundary line. The name Hey(e)s or Hayes has been adopted as a surname.

Combined with personal names, natural features have given us other place names. Simons-wood, Martins-croft, or mere, and Winstans-ley are examples of this.

Boundaries

Brooks form natural boundaries for the township.

Commencing at Golborne Hollows, Ellams Brook may be noticed. This provides the boundary between Golborne and Newton and eventually flows into Newton Mere.

The boundary between Golborne and Haydock runs from Newton by way of Dean Dam Farm through woodland, across to the White Doors Lodge, then along Sandy or Keeper's Lane, with Haydock Park racecourse on one side and Golborne on the other. Continuing from the end of Sandy Lane across farm land it reaches the Millingford Brook which has flowed from Billinge through Ashton. The brook winds its way through Golborne, later separating Golborne from Lowton. On reaching the Dale, the brook provides the division between Newton and the township, finally proceeding, like Ellams Brook, to the Mere. Long before the Mere was constructed, the brook was mentioned by Leland, the king's antiquary, 1533-59, in a reference to Newton: "a poore little market on a brooke."

Until this century Harvey Lane was devoid of houses except for a farmstead and two cottages in Hell Nook. Pedestrians had to splash through the brook until a narrow plank bridge was made at Ward's ford. This continued until 1930 when the long expected roadway between Edge Green and Harvey Lane was constructed and a substantial bridge was built.

Street Names

The first houses and shops were built along present High Street. As the population increased there was development northwards towards Wigan. The extended street became known as Church Street after the building of the parish church in 1849. Southwards, High Street became Bridge Street. At Town Farm on the outskirts of the township Bridge Street joined Park Road at the edge of Golborne Park. Town Farm bears the date 1740. It was here that Jane Pierpoint lived and allowed the nonconformists to worship in one of the farm buildings. Pierpoint Road leads to a seventeenth century farmhouse. An old mural is to be seen in one of its rooms.

Westwards from High Street a road led across the heath. One of Golborne's oldest inhabitants remembers the time when the shops in Heath Street near the Methodist chapel had front gardens. Where Bank Street and Barn Lane meet, Heath Street continued as Harvey Lane. Bank Street may have been named as the result of the Bank Heath Award. It leads to Edge Green by way of Edge Green Lane. Barn Lane, running in the opposite direction, took its name from one of Golborne's two old tithe barns.

The town's industrial developments are reflected in such names as Mill Lane, Tanner's Lane, Gas Street and Railway Road.

The Millingford Brook has given its name to one of the roads of a new housing estate.

Salisbury Street was named after Lord Salisbury, the prime minister, and Legh Street after the lord of the manor. Property speculators gave their names to other streets. Mr Barton kept the off-licence where Barton Street and Heath Street join. He built the first two houses down Barton Street. He also maintained and drove the hearse, or shillibier as it was then called, when it was needed for burials at Winwick church. With the further growth of the town various avenues have been named after persons important in local administration. This is how Caunce Avenue, Prescott, Twist, Naylor and Barrowdale roads came to be named.

Golborne Copp

This one time eminence conspicuous in 1660 and marked on the maps of 1774 is situated near Park Road. Whether it was an observation post or land mark is not known. The County History records that "besides the mound called Castle Hill in Newton, there are several interesting remains of similar character though smaller in dimension. One of these, a well marked circular barrow about 10 yards in diameter and five in height, stands close to the left of the highway leading from Edge Green to Golborne."

As there were only two ways from Edge Green, those of Sandy Lane and Barn Lane, the latter is the more likely, for it was close to the site of the Copp which was situated immediately behind the present residence known as The Heights.

Another mound is about one third of a mile away on Haydock land and is known as The Seven Sisters. There is no known evidence that this mound was a barrow but for what other purpose it may have been designed is not known either. The copp is not comparable with a South African copje or cop, for the height is relatively small. If archery was practiced, no mention is made of it, though it could be that such matters were so familiar to the few residents they did not consider it was necessary to refer to them. By statute of Edward IV it was decreed "that every Englishman should have a bow of his own height and that butts for the practice of archery should be erected in every village." The inhabitants were obliged to shoot up and down every feast day and were under penalty for non-compliance. During the time of the Tudors, trained bands of bowmen were established in most townships, Golborne had to find six such men, and Lowton a similar number. The copp was a suitable place for practice for on either side was the open heath. This, and another at some distance, is commonly called Robin Hood's Butts.

Nearby was the local bowling alley and possibly a green for Roger Lowe makes this entry in his diary: "I went to Golborne Cop to see a game bowled, came home again." Bowling in the alley was distinguished from bowling on the green. In the alley the bowls were circular discs. Again he writes "I went to the alley and played bowles'. The bowling resort and the bowl house were immediately behind the residence known as Brook Villa and the house referred to as Copp House.

The short road leading off Park Road by the side of Brook Villa still retains the name Bow Alley. A little distance away there used to be shallow pits known as the bow pits. The term bow is a shortened version of bowl suggested by the bowling alley. There remain within the district numerous similar pits.

Helen's Nook

According to some of the old maps the place known as Helen's Nook should be Hell Nook. How the name originated is a matter of speculation. There are several stories alluding to it. Tradition says it was the abode of the district nurse named Helen who lived in a small cottage there, well away from the highway. Such women were well known and were as much in demand as the doctor, probably more so.

Another suggestion is that when open-air services were held, rowdies made a practice of journeying from place to place to break them up. Possibly the worshippers, tired of "turning the other cheek" set upon the disturbers with such violence that the place was "like a nook of hell" while the fight lasted.

The Hollows

On the outskirts of the town Golborne Hollows, with its woods and stream, is one of the pleasantest parts of the township. Although a delightful place by day, it can be an eerie spot by night. A well-known medical man, Dr Worsley, told me of a startling experience he once had in this lonely place. Always fastidious about his dress and his meticulous flowing beard, he seldom appeared in public without a silk hat. Returning from a visit about midnight and coming through the Hollows in the stillness he detected a slight rustling movement in the foliage overhead. He stopped, wondering what it might be. Suddenly a hairy body dropped from the trees on to his shoulders. He was astonished. In alarm he clutched his topper and ran to the crest of the hill, meanwhile conscious of a warm, hairy body, active and chattering, attached to him. In desperation he whisked off his hat and immediately the creature dropped to earth and made off into the woods. What the animal was he did not then know. Next day he learned that a travelling organ grinder who had been touring the village had caused no small commotion because his monkey had escaped.

On the brow of the hill is a carriage way leading to Golborne Hall and Park. Banks of rhododendrons when they are in full bloom along the drive give an added beauty to the place. The hall has seen many changes. Rev. Ashburnham Legh of Golborne Parks, Mr Pearson, former High Sheriff of the County, Mr Drayton Grimpkie, managing director of Messrs. Evan's Ltd., Mr Catterall, cotton manufacturer, and various others have lived there. Another entrance to the park is by the Warrington Road Lodge. Many years ago most of the land on the Golborne Dale side, now bounded by a wall, was used for arable cropping and some excellent grain was produced. The roadway to the hall was fenced off, with open ditches left on either side. These ditches were largely responsible for the extinction of a local band. The township at the time had two bands. One practiced in a disused shed near The Inglewoods described as Crompton's band room; the other practiced at one of the inns near the centre of the town. Mr Pearson was then in residence at the hall, and toward the end of the year the first mentioned band, also called the Temperance Band - although the satirical pseudonym Buttermilk Band had been applied to it - had gone there to play. The night was very dark, and during the interval between going and returning, a dense fog descended. On the return journey the musicians lost their way. They became separated from one another. Some rambled off to the open land. Others had the misfortune to fall into the ditches which were well filled with water, and many lost their instruments. Whether these were afterwards recovered we cannot say, but the company did not survive the loss and no attempt appears to have been made to re-establish a second band in the town. About the Parkside Mills Band, possibly the first of its kind in Golborne, little information is available.

Like many other similar residences, much of the hall has been taken down. For a time, before the advent of the motor-car, the place attained distinction as a well known hackney stud farm. It has since become the headquarters of the Haydock Park Golf Club. Members formerly played on Haydock land but, owing to a change of circumstances, they moved to the Golborne site though they retained the old title.

Chapter III
Agriculture
The Bank Heath Award, 1763

Until the nineteenth century most of Golborne's inhabitants were directly or indirectly dependent upon the land for their livelihood. Hence agriculture played an important part in its history.

The enclosure of land in Golborne which took place in 1763 was perhaps the event which most affected the people as far as agricultural developments are concerned. This is a subject around which there has been much controversy. Arguments for and against have been vigorously stated, but if we are considering the greatest good to the greatest number of people, then the enclosures were beneficial.

In his *Short History of the English People*, Mr J.R. Green remarks that "the numerous enclosure Bills which appeared in the reign of George II and especially marked that of his successor, changed the whole face of the country. Ten thousand square miles of untilled land have been added under their operation to the area of cultivation, while in the tilled land itself, the production has been more than doubled by the advance of agriculture which began with the travels and treatises of Mr Arthur Young."

Young was a man of financial means who started his career as a farmer. Though some of his farming ventures failed, in 1768 he wrote a book describing his farming methods. Later, in 1784, he started a monthly magazine *The Annals of Agriculture*. When the Board of Agriculture was formed in 1793 he was appointed its first secretary. Young was an ardent supporter of enclosures although later he confessed that many hardships had accrued from them. He advocated outright ownership of land as that was the best security of tenure.

Sheer necessity was forcing enclosure upon the country, for without it there could be no improvement of live-stock or increased cereal production. The old strip system of land cultivation had to be abolished and the common land put to better use than fattening a few geese and an odd cow or two if England's increasing population was to be fed.

From 1700 to 1845 fourteen million acres of land were enclosed, and over fifteen hundred enclosure acts, including private ones, were passed. The cottagers and small holders who had enjoyed turf rights, rights of common, grazing rights and other rights, were deprived of these advantages. They suffered considerably, although their deprivations may have been exaggerated.

On the eve of enclosure the township had upwards of two hundred acres of heath and waste, a great proportion of which lay between Edge Green and Golborne Park. No one person was prepared to undertake its reclamation, for it required financial outlay far beyond what it was then worth to clear off the scrub and heath, to break it up, to drain and fence it.

As in other villages at this time, an Act of Parliament was required before the land could be enclosed. Such an act provided for the appointment of commissioners to make the necessary arrangements for the re-allocation of the land in accordance with people's claims.

Following an Act of 1763 The Bank Heath Award was made by three commissioners, the same persons who were responsible for the Lowton Heath Award. They were Samuel Johnson of Little Legh, Cheshire; Henry Porter of Rufford and Thomas Hawkshead of Heskin. Richard Orford of Haydock was collector of dues.

The Award commences: *Agreement, August 25th 1763 between Peter Legh of Lyme, Lord of the Manor of Golborne, and the Rev. Ashburnam Legh of Golborne Parks, Clerk, and Thomas Blackburn of Hale, John Legh of Outrington in the County of Chester, Legh Masters, of Newhall within Ashton, Rev. Robert Master of Croston, Francis Bryan, Clerk, of Golborne, Ralph Legh, George Birchall, Hugh Stirrup, Thomas Wilmott, Edward Rigg, Richard Birchall, Thomas Guest, Joseph Pott, Joshua Potts, John Leather, Margaret Cheetham, Thomas Evanson, Joseph Foster, Edward Pierpoint, Benjamin Banks, Thomas Fernhead, Thomas Pimblett, owners and proprietors, and several tenants.*

Peter Legh, the Lord of the Manor and also member of Parliament, is stated to be the owner of the soil and freehold of several large commons and waste ground within the Manor. Several of the parties are stated to have rights of common for one or more lives; some have pasture rights. Some rights of common are "subject to the land being unenclosed... of no profit or advantage, but capable of great improvement if divided and enclosed and tilled..."

The Award indicates that the several parties were willing and desirous that "all the said common and waste ground (except Edge Green) should be severed, divided, enclosed and allotted." Further, the people agree that "not only highways, but all proper ways shall be stopt and diverted by such ways and means as the law required... The referees shall settle who, and in what manner, and at whose expense, all hedges, ditches, gates, stiles and fences, be made in and about the enclosure."

It is provided that "all new highways, etc. set out, shall for ever after the making and setting out, be repaired and amended by the inhabitants of the township of Golborne...." It is ordered that "there shall be set apart, left open unoccupied, one acre of the said commons and waste grounds, in some convenient part thereof, for the getting of stone, sand and clay for the making of brick for the use of the township in their publick and private roads, and also for the private use of every inhabitant who shall use the same in the township of Golborne, and shall set apart and leave a convenient road to the same for the purpose thereof."

"The enclosed lands do contain 170 acres or thereabout... Divers small plots and inconsiderable strips or parcels of ground have been fenced off and enclosed from other parts of the commons and waste, without having the same assigned to them... They shall make payment for the enclosures, one shilling for every customary acre, and so on in proportion for every greater or lesser quantity of land enclosed."

A list is given of the smallholders and it appears they were paid for these lands, sums ranging from £36 to a few shillings, "in full satisfaction and compensation for their several interests." It was also ordered that a copy of the Award was to be kept by the Chapel Warden of St. Luke's, Lowton, and kept in safe custody in the Church Chest."

It would be interesting to learn how, and by whom, these privileges allowed to the inhabitants of Golborne have been permitted to disappear.

Field Names

The consideration of enclosures leads naturally to the study of field names. The naming of the fields in this and other townships served a very practical purpose and in several ways can be regarded as a part of our unwritten history. Many names when interpreted reveal an appropriate human interest which appears to fit into the life of the people who used them. Not only were the fields named, they were measured and subject to tithe and later to rates.

Fortunately, an interesting document relating to the year 1833 has been preserved. This *Survey and Valuation of the Township of Golborne, taken for equalizing the rates*, was prepared by R. Penswick of Ashton. It includes the names of the principal occupiers of land and houses and gives a complete list of the two hundred and fifty fields named, measured and valued for rating purposes. Generally they are of small acreage, mostly

A picture postcard showing the pride of Golborne.

under six acres. The name of the occupier is stated but we are left to puzzle out the locality of his holding. A few descendants of old time residents, familiar with the names, have been able to establish the situation of some.

As a result of this valuation the rates were increased by 4/6d in the pound for farm buildings, and 3/4d in the pound on cottage property. This was agreed by the landowners and lay-payers of the said township, and voted upon and instituted on 4 June, 1838. Again in 1858, according to the minutes of the Parish Council, "the third notice is hereby given that a meeting of the ratepayers of the parish of Golborne will be held in the old school on Thursday, December 9, 1858 at six o'clock in the evening for the purpose of considering the best method of revising the Rate Book of the same Parish."

The rateable value of Golborne in 1854 was stated to be £5564.12.2 and the population 2000; in 1901, £31,010 and in 1953, £35,968... but as the combined townships of Culcheth, part of Glazebury, Kenyon and Lowton are now included with Golborne, the combined rateable vale by 1954 was £79,707.

At the time of the 1833 survey the principal owners of land were the Banks, Birchalls, Caunces, Fosters, Squire Legh, the Potts, Pierpoints, Streets and Worsleys. Only a few farmers occupied over a hundred acres. Jas. Livesley farmed 160 acres. The brothers Pimblett jointly held 174 acres, Jane Pierpoint 100 acres, Andrew Caunce 115 acres.

Considering that most of the occupied land has passed to various tenants, it is doubtful if, in any instance, any relative of the occupiers of land in 1833 remains.

Many nooks, heys and crofts appear in the survey. Bowling Alley Croft is connected with the Bowling Alley mentioned by Roger Lowe near the Copp. Clayford Lane may belong to Barn Lane, because clay pits and kilns are situated nearby. There was a ford there similar to the one in Harvey Lane, where there were also clay pits and brick-kiln.

33

Whereas Ordnance maps and numbers meet the requirements of a modern age, names such as Bessey's Meadow, Granny's Field and Parlour Field relate to a quieter and more homely period with a warm and personal, almost affectionate, association. True, there were mischievous people for we are aware of incidents arising from the nocturnal ramblings of the ghost and boggart. Boggart Pit and Boggart Field are reminders of the past which also included the Bear Ring and the Turnpike although we await proof of the whereabouts of these places.

Nuts, wild apples and blackberries were abundant, for there was Bramberry Field, Hazlers Hey (enclosure), Crabtree Nook, together with such names as Daisy Field, and Trefoil Field. Other names refer to a way of life, for there are many marl heys and pits, lime kilns and brick crofts, although like the Brickmakers Arms these no longer exist. Mr Brewis, who built considerable cottage property, a new mill and school, is credited with having procured the bricks from local kilns.

Tan houses and tan pits were quite common in surrounding districts, and it is quite probable we had a small tan pit which may account for Tanners Lane. There was a lime kiln not very far away from the old pipe shop where one Henry Birchall, was concerned with the making of clay pipes, particularly churchwarden pipes.

Payment of Tithe

Closely related to the holding of Land was the payment of tithe. This is a subject which goes far beyond local history, and was discussed by Greeks, Carthagians, Hebrews and others. The subject is interesting but it is beyond our purpose to discuss its origin.

It is an established fact that in 1650 the township paid tithe to the value of £35 and that in 1837 in the sister township of Lowton tithe was paid both in money and in kind. One of the principles laid down as a basis was that "things taken from the earth", grain, fruits and herbage, should be subject to tithe. Secondly, "things maintained by the earth", lambs, calves, colts, fowl, milk, cheese, eggs and the like: thirdly, things arising from profits in the pursuit of trade, occupations and professions were subject to tithe. It should not be assumed that tithes were paid solely to the clergy; land-owners also claimed them. In a will dated 1546 certain monies, and the

34

tithes of Lowton and Hulme were donated to a beneficiary under the said will. The tithe referred to "corne, hemp and flax". (Warrington at the time was celebrated for the manufacture of ropes and sailcloth).

We have been accustomed to regard tithe as a tenth part of something and our curiosity is quickened when we are faced with the fact that in the payment of corn, it was the eleventh sheaf that was taken. Confirmation of this custom, still operating in 1837, is given in *The Survey of Agriculture* (1795) in this neighbourhood. In it is stated: "The tythe collected was one eleventh of corn, and for meadow hay 5/- an acre, and for best hay 6/- an acre." Lowton paid one penny for a house, three pence for man and wife, five shillings for a calf; if no calf, then three half pence for a calving cow, and a penny for a barren one. Pigs and lambs were tithed at two shillings and sixpence; for every colt a shilling; for a goose two pence; wool was tithed by every tenth sheep, or one tenth of the whole clip.

A Cheshire acre of potatoes paid eight shillings and sixpence, and mortuaries were payable according to the statute acre. Several inconsistencies are perceptible and to some extent payment would have depended upon the honesty of the payer. Where the clergy had to collect tithes it must have been a comfortless and vexatious task.

We have not been able to secure any information about a tithe map. No doubt if one is found it will be similar to the one for the adjoining parish of Lowton dated 1837.

Two tithe barns are said to have been built for the convenience of those who paid tithe in kind. One was situated in Barn Lane, the other on land near to where the parish church now is.

Agriculture During The War Years

Local history is incomplete without some reference to food production, especially during the war years. It was in the First World War, 1914-18, that we awoke to the fact that our food supplies were in jeopardy. We had been so accustomed to relying on a cheap overseas supply that no provision had been made to counteract such contingencies as resulted from war. A few thoughtful persons foresaw the possibility of starvation and misery. A publication, which is quite a revealing document, had been issued dealing with the progress of German agriculture showing how far ahead Germany was of this country in food production, in spite of poorer soil. Only after the war had been in progress for one and a half years did we appreciate the necessity of formulating a policy. So it was decided to divide the country into districts and to set up advisory committees. The districts were to include adjoining townships each with a representative to report to the district executive. Golborne was included in the Wigan district, along with nineteen other townships, and was expected to report on a total of 22,000 acres of arable land. It was not until March 1916 that these newly appointed committees settled down to work and along with other districts reported to the County Executive Committee at Preston.

Earl Selborne had been appointed to the presidency of the Board of Agriculture (not yet raised to the status of a ministry) and all county committees reported to the Board. The Wigan committee was composed of estate agents, landlords, land valuers, tenant occupiers and owners, and was thoroughly representative. As might well be expected, some breezy exchanges of opinion ensued. As an introduction, the committee had before it a letter from the Board drawing the attention of the districts to "the destruction of noxious weeds and a review of wet areas," together with an unusual request asking the committee "to devise ways and means for the inspection of farms producing less than the average of foodstuffs in the district." It was tantamount to saying: "We are in a difficulty and we ask you to find a solution."

Such a request was nothing less than a confession of weakness. There was nothing challenging about it, nothing constructive, especially as the committee were "to devise ways and means." Eventually a resolution was drawn up, and it was agreed that it should be sent to the President of the Board as well as to the County Executive.

The resolution stated:-

The Committee recognise that some land may at present not be producing near its maximum. The cause may be with the landlord or the farmer, or cumulative, the whole combined. It cannot be expected that a voluntary statement will be made either by the owner or the occupier of the land, nor can it be expected that neighbours will voluntarily sit in judgment or become informers of such cases. This is a matter of NATIONAL IMPORTANCE and the responsibility for obtaining the information should be undertaken by the Board.

We make the following recommendations:-

1. That the Returns now sent out on the fourth of June should be obligatory, showing the stocking and cropping of each farm and small holding.

2. As soon as the Returns have been received, inspectors should be empowered to visit all such farms as disclose insufficient production. That the inspectors shall be men of practical experience and shall report the result of the enquiry to the County Executive Committee; the Committee to formulate such remedies as may seem necessary. Those requiring legislation, to be forwarded to the Board of Agriculture, others capable of being dealt with by negotiation should be dealt with by the Committee.

During the year 1916 Earl Selborne resigned from the Board and was succeeded by Mr Prothero (later Lord Ernle), who in January, 1917 issued a letter to County Committees informing them that "by an Order in Council under the Defence of the Realm Act certain powers have been conferred on the Board with the object of maintaining the food supply of the country." The powers were extensive. The June Returns became compulsory. Hitherto, if a person chose he could neglect or refuse to complete them, and as a result the government's information had been incomplete. A survey of the land took place and many recommendations were made. Some were approved and carried out, others dragged wearily on to the termination of the war, and in some instances land was left in a poor condition until the outbreak of the Second World War.

A glimmer of hope appeared with the Corn Production Act but it soon flickered out. As if this was not enough, to frustrate our efforts in the inter-war years, we had the bounty-fed corn, corn subsidised by the German Government, to contend with. This brought about a ruinous state of affairs for the arable farmer with crippling effects on the land-owner from which many have never fully recovered.

Here we must leave the facts to speak for themselves. Suffice it to say that on the outbreak of hostilities in 1939, within two days, preparations were in hand for an intensive food drive embracing practically the whole of the plans introduced in the 1914-18 campaign. As time progressed, many of the powers were considerably reinforced.

A new survey of farm land took place. Not only had it to be ploughed and cropped, but field drainage and water courses had to be cleared. Pasture land was to be cropped without an occupier being penalised by restrictive clauses in his tenancy agreement. Farms ware classified as A, B or C, plus or minus. The incompetent tenant or occupier, even though he owned the land, could not do as he wished, and either had to make a decided improvement or give place to some approved person. After the end of the war new terms of tenure were discussed and these terminated in additional security for a worthy tenant under the provisions of the 1947 Agricultural Holdings Act. Land is far too precious to waste and all occupiers should be obliged to prove their ability to use it efficiently, and not merely occupy it for sentimental or less worthy reasons.

Results have proved that we can, and are able to, produce more and better crops; that cattle and other livestock can be bred and maintained efficiently using our own resources, that better grasses, cereal and other crops are being introduced, and that we are on the verge of a new age. The plant breeder, biologist, chemist and engineer are playing a more important part than ever before in the production of our daily bread.

Agricultural Pioneers: The Garton Brothers

Dean Swift gave it as his opinion that "whosoever could make two ears of corn or two blades of grass grow upon a spot of ground where only one grew before, would deserve better of mankind and do more essential service to his country than the whole race of politicians put together."

Such services were rendered by Robert and John Garton, members of a local family, who won fame in the world of agriculture by producing new and better varieties of seeds and plants.

As the area of land available for cultivation in this island diminishes, the production of food must be increased by scientific plant breeding. The initiative and research of the Garton brothers have contributed greatly to this. Robert Garton, son of Mr Peter Garton was born at Helen's Nook,

A History of Golborne

Golborne in February 1858. Some years later, the family took over the tenancy of Dean Dam Farm, and it was there that the brothers Robert and John developed their plant breeding experiments. Robert Garton was primarily responsible for the early ventures. These were developed later by John Garton whose scientific training proved invaluable to the scheme.

In those early years it was generally believed that the florets of cereals were, like many other plants, naturally cross pollinated, the pollen being carried by the wind or insects from one floret to another. Having proved that this was not so, the next step was the crossing of distinct varieties in several classes to produce new breeds possessing greater yields, greater strength in the straw and earlier maturity than the varieties then grown.

Like many other discoveries the ideas were received with apathy and indifference. When the new oat Abundance was introduced its sensational arrival did not immediately receive recognition. In fact, John Garton wanted to hand his discoveries over to the state and to free himself for further research, but the state was not interested. This may have been a blessing in disguise, for the brothers thereupon decided to commercialise their interests and the business of R & J Garton commenced in 1880.

Some years later, a younger brother joined the partnership and in 1896 the company of Gartons Ltd. the originators of scientific seed breeding, became incorporated.

From his youth upwards, John Garton devoted his leisure to the study of scientific subjects. He became absorbed in the investigation of the reproduction of farm plants. The discoveries which he made are now world famous. His abilities as a bacteriologist were exceptional. Acting with other members of his family, as early as 1900 they established, and later permanently endowed, the course of lectures on Colonial and Indian development which bears his name.

This munificent gift was made as a thank offering for the recognition and sympathy extended to John Garton's early efforts in the botanical and Agricultural departments of Edinburgh University at a time when there was little public acknowledgment.

Unfortunately, when John died prematurely in May 1922, the agricultural world lost one of its greatest benefactors and science a brilliant investigator. Had he lived there would have been conferred upon him at the graduation ceremony in July the Honorary Degree of Ll.D., which was posthumously awarded.

Owing to an ever-increasing expansion of business and the necessity of having adequate grounds for experimental purposes, the company established their own farms and additional testing grounds. The most rigorous tests, extending over a period of years, were applied to all new breeds of wheat, oats, barley and root crop seeds. In fact, the large number of new breeds of cereals now under scrutiny "is far beyond that attained by any other Plant Breeding Station."

Like Nature careful of the type
And finding that of fifty seeds
She often brings but one to bear,

so the most meticulous care must be taken regarding these new creations in plant life before reliability is assured. It reminds us of the American genius Luther Burbank, who has done so much to introduce new fruits and flowers, such as the stoneless plum, the spineless cactus, the plumcot; thousands of new breeds were burned before the fixed type was assured.

It was stated in the *North British Agriculturalist* that "Gartons have rendered a service which the country can hardly ever repay. Many of the heavy cropping varieties of grain which have helped the country through its recent troubles were of their introduction."

When the late Secretary of the U.S.A. Board of Agriculture, W.M. Hayes, himself a plant breeder, paid an official visit of enquiry to Europe, visiting plant breeding stations on the Continent and reviewing what had been done in this country, in America and Canada, he stated that "without any question of doubt Garton's work in value and importance exceeded all the work of all the other investigators put together."

Thus Golborne has its links with notable people for the originators of scientific plant breeding were Golborne people.

An early picture of Golborne Co-operative

The Farm House of the Past

Every township in the Hundred had its manor house, or hall; some are of special interest. Dr. Kurden writing of the Baron's Castle at Newton says: "On the left hand, close to a water mill are the ruins of the site of an ancient barony of Newton, formerly a baron's castle. Presumably this was the one time residence of Sir Thomas Langton. The site mentioned would be near the present picturesque Newton Hall, built by Sir Thomas Blackburn in 1634, (This was pulled down in 1959). No other place in the township was suited to use a water mill, and a mill, now in a ruinous state, is close by. There were numerous other halls - Lightshaw, Abram, Bryn, Bamfurlong, Byrom, Haydock, Southworth, Middleton, Bradley and Garswood. In Golborne were Grimshaw Hall and a yeoman's residence The Heywoods. Several halls had private chapels.

These halls and farm houses were of necessity self-contained units, capable of withstanding a siege for weeks on end. Roads during the winter were almost impassable. Markets, shopping and transport being negligible, flour and meal were stored by the sackful. In the farm houses, bread was usually baked twice a week in the old fashioned brick oven. Clap bread (oatcakes), throdkins, brewis, whey, beastings, formed part of the diet as occasion served. The housewife attended to the brewing - hence the name brewster - for home brewed ale was the usual beverage. Reserves of hams and bacon were essential. Cheese and butter making began to decline locally about 1870. Buttermilk, a by-product, was much sought after by those who kept pigs. The commodious cellars were well stocked with pickled beef and salted pork for the approaching winter. Salting stones, brick ovens and querns are relics of the past and, like turnspits, tinder boxes and goffering irons are now more or less curiosities.

Most farm houses had an oak corner cupboard, a grandfather clock, oak chest and brass or copper warming pans. The spinning-wheel and the hand loom were part of the furnishings. Bedsteads - many of them huge affairs raised several feet above the floor - had a canopy and curtains, and the beds, according to circumstances, were made of feathers, chaff or leaves. Waste fats from the kitchen provided material for rush lights. Soap and candles were home-made. Honey was in plentiful supply, and was used for the curing of meat as well as for sweetening purposes. Apples and other fruits were stored or preserved. Raspberries, whinberries, blackcurrants, blackberries and gooseberries served for cordials; it was a poor household that could not provide hospitality in the nature of elderberry or blackberry wine.

We rarely hear of rose wine now although at one period rose petals and violet leaves were chopped, stewed and eaten. My informant described how his mother used to make a delicious wine from the petals of roses. Only white ones were gathered and placed in a pan. Boiling water, sugar, and some other ingredients which he did not remember were added. Remembering the delectable qualities of the wine he added with gusto "Aye mon, an' it wur tackle." The housewife also had her herbarium and concocted syrups and simples; parsley tea for rheumatism, dandelion for liver complaints, coltsfoot for asthma, ragwort for poultices, and eyebright for eye troubles. Comfrey (nip-bone) was preserved in liberal quantities as it was the general remedy for sprains. Sage, thyme, rosemary and mint were used for sauces and forcemeat, while seasonal drinks were made from nettles and dandelions.

The growing of gooseberries and other bush fruit appears to have become something of a hobby. Several clubs have been traced in the neighbourhood and, according to the booklets published, the berries - both the green and red varieties - must have been of remarkable size. In a way the clubs were the fore-runners of horticultural shows, and members were encouraged to grow such produce. The Rev. H. Kirkpatrick of Park Lane, Ashton (1738-1799) was keenly interested in the growing of bush fruits and offered several varieties for sale.

A survey of the district shows the site of a small garden where bush fruit was grown, as well as numerous orchards; only a few now remain. This could be because, when the British Alkali industry commenced at St. Helens in 1822, hydrochloric acid fumes were allowed to escape into the air and extensive damage was done to crops of all kinds for miles around. The trees suffered and the damage done to fruit trees in particular was so extensive that numerous orchards simply disappeared.

It was not until 1838 that William Gossage invented a method for absorbing the destructive gases, but by that time the damage was irreparable. Similar results have been experienced as a result of the objectionable fumes rising from colliery dirt heaps. Cereal crops have suffered greatly. Some of the growers of grain crops did not have the means to take legal action against offending companies and suffered accordingly. In later years, however, when unity of action became possible, offending companies have been compelled to pay adequate compensation.

The Rev. H. Kirkpatrick, as well as growing fruit, also published a booklet on the cultivation of potatoes in Lancashire and Cheshire. Several present day practices relating to the growing of potatoes, such as the sprouting of the tubers, were being tried in his day. In the *Minutes of Agriculture,* Marshall states: "With a common ivory scoop about half an inch in diameter I drew out the eyes of large potatoes." Other records show that it was not unusual in 1790 to sprout tubers in this district and cut out the eyes with a portion of the potato and spread them on the floor of a room, then cover them with oat shudes or sawdust as protection against frost.

All doors and windows were kept open during the day except in frosty weather. Change of seed from Scotland, brought by boat to Liverpool was also practised. Planting in drills was known, though butts were in general use.

Lancashire is stated to have been the first county in the kingdom in which the potato was grown and was described in 1795 as standing unrivalled in the superior cultivation of this crop.

COUNTRY CHARACTERS

THE CRAFTSMEN OF THE FIELDS

Observant people are acutely conscious of the ever diminishing area of land in this island and the problem before us is how to produce more food from a smaller acreage. For this reason recognition should be given primarily to the ploughman and the drainer, for they are craftsmen whose work is at the foundation of our food supply, although they have often been denied the recognition they so richly deserve.

John Ruskin paid them a heartening tribute when he said: "Teach the plough exercise as carefully as you do the sword exercise, and let the officers of the troops of life be as much gentlemen as the officers of the troops of death."

Illustrations taken from the Lutrell psalter represent some of the ancient methods of tillage. The ploughman was not only expected to repair his ploughs and harrows, he was also expected to make them. The iron cutting parts, the coulter and share, no doubt were made by the smith, but all else was made of wood; even the plough breast was made of smooth-grained wood, and these wooden mould-boards are known to have been in use here in the nineteenth century.

Before the Enclosure Acts were passed the method employed in the ploughing of land was that generally used in the old open field strip system, where each occupier held strips each equivalent to the area a team of oxen could plough in a day. Usually each strip was one acre and the ploughing of that was regarded as a day's work. Twenty different occupiers of the common land could hold twenty separate strips and each strip was separated from its fellow by the trench furrow. The method employed in the ploughing was to follow the slope of the land, and surface drainage consequently followed the line of the furrow. Only in special circumstances was it considered wise to plough across the slope. Hence the skill of the craftsman was manifest in his ability to lay out the land in a manner suited to take water off it by surface drainage. The drainer, by contrast instead of taking water off the land, took the water out of the land. Several hundreds of acres in the county were improved and extensive areas of bog, moss, moor and waste were brought into cultivation, although the operation was a costly one. Some remarkable results were attained, for it has been said that "the art of taking levels was at first considered above the capacity of country surveyors." We pass over many silent centuries to the later part of the eighteenth century before we learn about effective drainage. When Arthur Young visited Lancashire in 1770 he wrote: "I forgot to tell you about a few sensible farmers in Lancashire who have come of late into the way of making hollow drains for the improvement of wet land. They lay two bricks on edge and one on top. Digging and laying cost fourpence a rood." The price of brick was then 10/- per thousand and a brick tax was added of 5/- per thousand. Holt confirms these findings.

By the middle of the nineteenth century the government were prepared to make loans available at a reasonable rate of interest. The old methods have now been superseded and results are being achieved by craftsmen of a new order. Whilst acknowledging our indebtedness to the achievements of the past, we know that its doors are closed against us and we cannot go back again.

Bullocks were to be seen in 1880 ploughing Golborne land. Now the horse is rarely seen and, with the single furrow plough, will soon be a feature of the past. The machine has displaced it, and like the peasantry in *The Deserted Village* once destroyed, it can never be revived. With the disappearance of the horse for ploughing there is not the same need for the shoeing forge, and in many instances the smith has disappeared, together with the hames and chain maker, the saddler, collar-maker, wheelwright and wagon builder.

As late as 1880 there was to be found in most of the houses on Ashton Heath a smith's hearth. Chain-making, the making of iron nails and locks was general. No doubt something similar was to be found at the Golborne smithies in Smithy Lane.

Before the age of the veterinary surgeon the smith served under the name of farrier. For numerous presumed ailments bleeding was resorted to. According to custom, "on St.Stephen's Day all horses should be bled." The farrier practiced docking, drenching, balling and blistering. If a horse had an offending tooth and was unable to eat, the service of the farrier was sought.

Although the pain might be excruciating there were no anaesthetics when the tooth came to be extracted. The treatment may appear brutal but there was no other way but to blindfold the horse, force open its mouth and knockout the offending tooth with a hammer and chisel.

According to Mr Holt's account: "Horse surgery under Mr Moorcroft and by the establishment of a veterinary college seems to be making rapid progress towards a perfection unknown in other countries."

Craftsmanship appeared in the work of the hedger. With the coming of enclosures the open fields disappeared in the late eighteenth century, and the countryside became a countryside of hedges, enclosed fields and scattered farms as we know it today. Holt's review of this district made in 1795 for the Board of Agriculture records this rather startling feature; "the practice of planting hedges is almost unknown in this county." The development of the quickthorn fence brought into being the craftsman competent to fell and layer a fence and make it stock proof.

At the present time the hedgerows, once a cause for pride, are disappearing. In some places nothing remains except a boundary fence. Even the trees appear to be doomed by the short-sighted policy of would-be economists returning to the open fields of the past.

The Decline Of The Craftsman

The decline and passing of the old time craftsman is an event which many people deplore. To the present generation the craftsman is merely a memory; in the future he will be known chiefly from books. Yet though rural crafts are an absorbing interest we can here only present the subject in outline.

The skill of the builder, carpenter and smith is to be seen in a few remaining buildings where the principal roof timbers are fashioned in the rough from tree trunks with other timbers fastened with oak pegs, the whole strong enough to carry the flagged roofing material and durable still for years to come. The iron work of the smith is shown in the stout hinges, gudgeons and latches, many of them being set in stone work designed to withstand rough usage for ages. In those days men built for service and not merely for sale. They had pride in their work more than in the speed with which they could get rid of it.

Mr Massingham who has so often championed the cause of the craftsman, presents in his book *Country Relics* a picture of a kind of museum, wherein are assembled tools of every description used by the men of by-gone ages: the adze, the axe, the auger, the cross-cut saw used in the saw pits; tools of the dry stone waller, thatcher, hedger, drainer, basket-maker; the equipment of the lace maker - "pillows and bobbins, all her little store" ; and the well worn sickle side by side with the scythe and flail. There are also threshels, hoppets, shears, and numerous furnishings of the teamster and ploughman, with implements of wood and even the wooden plough breast of special design.

The practice of adapting an old building for the housing of obsolete tools and machines is spreading. Dibbles or setting sticks, butter prints and bowls, cheese presses, querns and a host of other tools are preserved, together with the handiwork of the smith and the woodcarver. All of this bespeaks a pride in workmanship now rapidly disappearing. Amongst local discoveries are samplers, tapestry, weaving and the like. Even a few exhibits of pottery have been found on which these lines were engraved:

> *Let the wealthy and the great*
> *Roll in splendour and state*
> *I envy them not I declare it.*
> *I eat my own lamb*
> *My chickens and ham*
> *I shear my own fleece and I wear it.*
> *I have lawns I have bowers*
> *I have fruits I have flowers*
> *The lark is my morning alarmer.*
> *So jolly boys now*
> *Here God speed the plow*
> *Long life and success to the farmer.*

Our own township at one time had two blacksmiths and two wheelwrights building carts, barrows, ladders, gates and the like. Carts were the principal means of conveyance for products of every description. The making of them would now be deemed slow but in those days, considering the amount of rough usage they endured and knowing the condition of the roads, it is a worthy testimony to the builders and their craftsmanship that their work lasted for sixty and more years. Oak and ash were the chief woods used. It was a pleasant sight to see the planks stored away in lofts, drying and maturing for years. Lurries were not seen in the district before 1870 and some of the early ones were built with a turntable much too small, so that in the event of turning the load was inclined to topple over. As the turntable difficulty of the lorry was overcome it soon became immensely popular. Being well sprung and having reliable brakes it was well adapted to the needs of the age.

A few of the older inhabitants have assured me that from their early years they remember as many as twenty carts at once proceeding to Wigan market laden with every kind of produce. Among the wheelwright celebrities we had one whose name was outstanding for reliable workmanship. Of the carts he made it used to be said that they were easy of draught, nicely balanced on the axle, and recognisable by the knock they made as they went along the road. Though unseen, it was usual to say of them: "Yon's one o' Owd Billy's carts: yo' can tell me um onny weer. They knock twice when they stop." Similar credit was given to the reliability of his wheelbarrows. The old wheelwright used to say: "If I make you a barrow to work a day and play a day, I'll make it of oak. If it has to work every day I'll make it of ash." Even after twenty-five years service owners took a pride in caring for them.

In farming, numerous changes have taken place, from using the sickle and sythe - in common use in the district in 1790 - to using the combine harvester. Undoubtedly there was a kind of poetry in motion in watching the sweep of the scythe as the mower laid the gold topped swathes in orderly sequence for the gatherer and binder of sheaves. A skilled craftsman could whet a scythe to keep an edge for an hour whereas a novice would need to sharpen it about four times in the same period.

In the days when craftsmen flourished, slogging away with a flail was an irksome task. When John Naylor of Ashton invented his threshing machine it was a primitive affair and cost five pounds. It required two men to turn it, one to feed it and a youth to carry away the straw. The grain was collected and winnowed by a portable machine for which the modest sum of sixpence a day was the hiring charge.

In all these matters we have to be realists, and while we pay every tribute to the skill and dependability of the craftsman we must realise that economic forces are driving us to change. Only a very few people, for example, are willing to pay an extra price for hand-sewn boots. Not many workers would care to spend a full day shearing sheep when the same work could be done in one hour with far more ease with a machine. Anyone who argues for a return of the former days would be in as great a dilemma handling the tools of the craftsman as the latter would in using tools of the modernist. Even a craftsman cannot live on sentiment and if he is to survive we at least must make it worth his while to do so. "For the work so made, be it good or bad, so is the maker of it." We cannot all revert to the past "and scorn delights and live laborious days" for sentimental reasons.

However, attempts are made to stimulate interest in declining crafts; exhibitions, lectures and competitions are arranged and these contests help to preserve and revive rural crafts. Several adjoining townships grouped themselves together and formed *The Lowton and District Ploughing Society* in 1883 to organise competitions. There were numerous craftsmen at the time in Winwick, Newton, Lowton, Hulme, Kenyon and Golborne who had taken part in the older Makerfield Society which had started about 1853 and still continues to be well patronised.

The first president of the District Society was Col. McCorquodale, High Sheriff of the County; W.H. Arnott Esq. J.P. was Vice-president. The first competition, said to have been well attended by visitors and ploughmen, took place on land adjacent to Lyme House, Lowton. The competitors, committee and guests later adjourned to a neighbouring inn for dinner and the distribution of prizes. It is such events that Arthur Bryant has described in *The Age of Elegance*: "In the ale-house, over mid-day cheese and ale in the fields, countrymen sang of their craft and skill, prizing them more for the singing.

> *Hold gard'ner, sang the ploughman, my calling don't despise*
> *Since each man for his living upon his trade relies.*
> *Were it not for the ploughman, both rich and poor would rue*
> *For we are all dependent upon the painful plough.*

It was among such songs the sentiment, honour, memory, poetry and robust coarseness of the race was voiced."

We have now entered a phase which gives additional prestige to this essential craft of ploughing. Competitions have been arranged on a wider basis. In November 1953 a national contest was held at Garswood Park, Ashton-in-Makerfield. This may prove to be a forerunner of a world-wide contest.

Such displays and contests have been promoted to induce a revival of rural crafts. Their success is limited. Though many would like the crafts to be preserved they may survive in the nature of a hobby rather than as a means of livelihood.

Other craftsmen - the thatcher and basket-maker - have almost disappeared. While considering the passing of the rural craftsman it may be expedient to ask if his present day successor is not equally a craftsman. He produces effective results under improved conditions much more quickly and with better tools. Soon, present-day accomplishments, like their predecessors, will belong to a past age.

Poachers

Poachers, like many of the old craftsmen, have largely disappeared. Reference has already been made to the barons of the Hundred who acquired privileges under the terms of fee warren and free warren. The law of the Middle Ages was that no one could, without licence, take beast or bird even on his own land. However, poaching was not unknown, and the forest laws were violated, as may be seen from the court records of such cases as those tried at Wigan in 1324 when enquiry was held concerning the taking of deer. Numerous Game Acts were passed to discourage poaching even in the nineteenth century.

According to Brian V. Fitzgerald, the Game Act of 1831 was passed, not because of the activities of the poacher, but as the outcome of the Enclosure Acts. Be that as it may, the Game Laws were largely exclusive except for the aristocratic few, and many a man, driven to desperation with hunger, "unlawfully entering upon land for the taking of a rabbit" was caught in the act and suffered imprisonment. Many a wily poacher had pitted his wits against those of the keeper in sheer bravado and sometimes eluded capture. Some of them appear to have taken a delight in the sport even though they may have paid dearly for it.

There was a time when the law permitted the setting in the woods of spring guns and man-traps strong enough to break a person's leg. Such contrivances did not make any discrimination between an innocent wanderer or the poacher. No doubt it was argued that the wanderer had no business in the woods. In the local woods man-traps were set for a period, although enquiry has revealed that no-one was ever caught in them. Towards the latter part of the nineteenth century they were prohibited.

So far as we are concerned, numerous changes have caused the activity of the local poacher to be curtailed. Many a desperate struggle has taken place during the night or early mornings and gangs of roughs have been broken up. A few wily poachers who prefer to act alone still survive. They are most artful in spotting a squatting hare.

In sheep dog trials the enthusiasm of observers has often been aroused by the intelligent response of the dogs to the master's whistle and signs. A poacher's dog is just as intelligent. I have seen the poacher and his dog stand on a hedge bank. He would talk to the dog, lift it to his shoulder and point in the direction of the hare. He would then put the dog down and make off in the opposite direction. The dog hunted around, found the hare and the pursuit began. Having caught it the dog then made off with it to where his master's accomplice was stationed. The dog responded to his whistle and both cleared off to an adjoining footpath as if nothing had happened. It requires skill to net a sitting hare in broad daylight. Having witnessed the same I have been surprised by the agility and craftiness of such poachers. Unless a pursuer is capable of running swiftly over ploughed land any hope of catching the miscreant is futile. One man I knew who had paid dearly for his indiscretions remained incurable to the last. He was a quiet fellow but prohibitions only encouraged him to commit further offences. Having gained his confidence, I prevailed upon him to relate some of his experiences. He chuckled with glee as he related the following: Several petty offences had been alleged against him but nothing had been proved. Still, he was under suspicion, and as gamekeepers had at times unexpectedly appeared as he traversed certain bye-ways, he naturally concluded they were out "to get him." On this particular occasion when walking along a little frequented road a keeper stepped out from behind some bushes and accosted him. As his coat appeared to bulge, evidently concealing something, the keeper said: "What have you got there? Let me see!" "Not likely," said the suspect, "you've no right to search me." "Well I'm going to; I've been suspecting you for a long time." Without more ado, the inquisitor made a dash for the fellow's pockets. That was just what Old Velvet Jacket wanted. Making a weak show of resistance he twisted and turned as if to break away, but the keeper had his hand in the suspect's pocket, and hugged and tugged for all he was worth. The old boy was thoroughly enjoying himself as he finished the story. His little eyes sparkled with fiendish delight he chuckled and chortled as he described the torture he inflicted on the keeper for the fellow had grasped no hare, but a hedgehog.

Gypsies

Gypsies have frequented the district for generations and have been more or less tolerated. Probably they were around as early as the thirteenth century for at that period the local fairs commenced and it was the practice of gypsies to attend such places travelling from fair to fair. Horse trading became a speciality among them, though such trade is now negligible. A small amount of trading continues, mainly in piebald ponies such as are frequently seen by the wayside camps. It is not unusual to see groups camping together on the commons and roadside places although a movement is on foot to exclude them altogether from their customary resorts.

Towards the close of the nineteenth century they regularly appeared in this district, hawking a garish assortment of paper flowers and fireplace screens. They soldered pots and pans and re-seated the familiar Billinge chairs at one time prevalent hereabout. It would be quite a long story to tell of their artifices. The true Romany considers himself in a class apart from the many we are accustomed to describe as gypsies. It is among this latter class we find those who are addicted to petty thefts, such as pilfering fencing timbers, prowling in the woods seeking osiers and hazel twigs for basket and peg making. When caught in the act they can become very abusive. Where companies are grouped together it is usual to find a few hounds. These dogs never bark at an intruder. The cooking pot contains many substantial foods for the gypsies are as adept at cookery as at concealment. Their primitive oven is a handy contrivance. They have an open fire with plenty of ash, and when the fire dies down the hot ashes are scraped aside and a hole dug into which the bird or rabbit is put. This is then covered over with ash and protected by a metal cover. All suitable ash having been raked over the place and the fire replenished the cooking proceeds slowly and to perfection. In a way they can give lessons to the litter lout for true gypsies never leave fur or feathers after them, and one never sees gaunt starved ponies or famished dogs. As for themselves they are quite capable of providing the necessities of life and if they cannot bargain, as a last resort, they pay; but action little short of a surgical operation is required to get money from a gypsy.

Pests Officers

During the Second World War the services of the pests officers were in frequent demand. The damage done by vermin and pests to crops is considerable and disease is carried and spread by rats and other vermin. In war-time, measures had to be taken to check such losses.

Although to many people the office of pest officer is something of an innovation that of sparrow-catcher is traceable to 1566 when it was the custom at parish meetings for the church wardens and six other parishoners to meet and assess a rate for the destruction of sparrows and other vermin and to appoint two honest and substantial persons of the parish to be distributors of the provisions "for the destruction of noyful fowls and vermin" and to offer rewards for the heads and eggs of certain birds and the heads of certain beasts all of which "are to be destroyed burned consumed and cut assunder in the presence of the said church wardens."

The Winwick registers of 1747 refer to the destruction of sparrows and the price of two pence a dozen being paid for their heads - provided that they had been caught in the Parish. The Lowton registers mention a halfpenny a head as being the price allowed. Sparrow-catchers used to travel about the district armed with nets and lamps. They tried the stacks of corn or hay and the eaves of buildings where they caught hundreds of birds. For some unknown reason in a near-by parish hedgehogs were included as vermin, and twopence a head was allowed for their destruction. Most likely the legendary story that these animals suck the milk from cows as they lie resting in the fields had been accepted as fact.

Burleymen

An official who has now disappeared was the burleyman. In the ancient laws of Lancashire and Cheshire reference is made to burleymen. "In the Honor and Fee of Makerfield in the Manor of Widnes in Lancashire as late as 1879 burleymen were appointed at the Court Leete and Baron. Men of agricultural experience were always chosen and their duty was to value crops damaged by straying cattle. A judge of the county court was in the habit of relying on their evidence and, by consent, referring cases to them."

We know that the Court Baron existed in Newton until 1884. Having met some of the appointed men I learned about the duties they performed. The term burleymen may be better understood as byre-law men the byre indicates the place for the housing of cattle. These men assessed damage done by straying cattle or other live stock. Generally such cases were settled out of court. Unless the owner was known stray cattle were usually impounded, and remained so until the legal charges had been paid. There is no record of any pound for the township. The one at Newton Rock is the nearest one known.

The Golborne authority from 1857 onward made various appointments such as those of surveyor, overseer of the poor, nuisance inspector and burleymen. All such appointments were made annually. Several of the burleymen - Richard Fearns, Edward Last, James Bridge, John Fearns and others were of well known local families. It is difficult to understand why the Court Baron should nominate burleymen to act within its own province and the Parochial Committee or Parish Council should also nominate its own officers. A minute in the Council records relates to the appointment made by the Parish Council and to the same being revoked by Order of the Court. No reason for this was given. Appparently such appointments were subject to confirmation. Had much valuable information not been mislaid, appropriated or destroyed, we might have seen more clearly how such decisions were arrived at.

55

Chapter IV
Industry - Coal Mining

Coal was used by the Romans and during the Anglo-Saxon period. Bede in his history mentions that "Wulfred should send each year to the monastery six loads of wood, twelve loads of coal, and six loads of peat."

In a deed in the Wigan Reference Library allusion is made to *fyrston ae cole* an outcrop of the Arley seam (1350).

Roger Lowe appears to have regarded a coal-mine in the nature of a curiosity for he makes this entry in his diary, April 1664: "John Haseldine and I went to his brother's ground to see a cole pitt." Apparently, this mine and others similar to it in the area was not very deep and few precautions against accidents appear to have been taken, for again he comments "There came a ladd to the cole pitt with a horse for coles and looking down he fell down and was killed. He was the son of Thomas Arrowsmith of Lowton Common."

Miss Celia Fiennes in her notes   *Passing through Wiggon* (1697) expressed surprise and interest "in the various   articles she saw there carved out of coal and offered for sale."

Almost one hundred years later, coal was being mined at Haydock. In the Bank Heath Award relating to the enclosure of land in Golborne mention is made of "an ancient road leading from Dean Dam to Haydock Colliery."

So far as the industry in Golborne is concerned the first mine appears to have been opened at Edge Green about 1825 by a Mr Critchley. The Edge Green mine must have been a shallow one for William Alexander mentions in his Itinerary visiting the place and reports "that singing could be heard proceeding from the mine." In those days, coals were carried up a ladder in corves; and later a horse-gin or windlass was used. The haulage rope was made of cotton and described as a cotton dandy and the shallow pits were known as dandy pits. A field in the vicinity bears the name Dandy Field.

In an attractive brochure published by Messrs. R. Evans and Co. a description is given of this company's origins and activities. The founder, Mr Richard Evans, a successful London publisher, appears to have considered giving up business. A life of complete retirement may not have appealed to him and he looked around for a sound investment. It is conceivable that the new railway from Liverpool to Manchester had attracted his attention. Report says that George Stephenson had obtained supplies of coal for his engine from the small mine at Edge Green, then owned by Mr Critchley. Mr Evans visited him, and as a result of the interview obtained an interest in the mine and eventually bought it. Next we find him, in 1833, acquiring the share held by Mr Legh of Lyme Hall in the firm of Legh & Turner, who at the time were working the Earthy, Potato and Florida seams at Haydock. The partnership continued until 1845 when Mr Evans bought out Mr Turner and founded the firm of Richard Evans & Co.

According to a note in the Athenaeum the company paid, presumably to Sir Robert Gerard, £5,000 a year and to W.J. Legh Esq. £4,000.

They owned twenty-five locomotives, wagons by the hundred, pits by the dozen, "houses and farms and buildings as though they were princes."

The Golborne Colliery started by Alderman Johnson of St. Helens about 1870 was also acquired by Evans & Co., and was worked by them for over twenty years before being re-organised in 1908. The winding shaft was then sunk to a depth of six hundred yards, and a tunnel 1400 yards long intersected various seams. The whole output could thereby be concentrated in one shaft. To work the scheme successfully electricity was necessary. This was the first instance of high tension current being applied to a colliery. In all there are now (1955) eighteen electrically driven haulages at work in the mine.

The powers range from 150 H.P. to 15 H.P. for auxiliary sets. The depth of the winding shaft is six hundred yards and is "one of the deepest of the company's mines." Other extensive operations were made: coal from the several mines was moved about the country by road, rail and canal. These local mines were connected with the Leeds-Liverpool canal at the Abram boundary by a light railway at a place locally known as the Bason.

In the *Memorials of Liverpool* (1875) it is significant to note that "large quantities of coal were shipped by the Sankey canal, and coal flats were pulled by men, six or eight abreast, yoked to a common rope because the local landowners had inserted a clause in the Bill which forbade the use of horse power."

Details of a few other incidents of minor importance have been collected. In one of the Edge Green mines the first local mining sensation occurred. Water broke through from a mine known as the Old Pumping Pit. Fortunately, the miners escaped but lost all their tools and the pit ponies were drowned. The mine was closed and no attempt was ever made to re-open it. A somewhat unusual story is related in connection with one of these shallow mines. Several of the older inhabitants have been closely questioned and all agree upon the truthfulness of the incident. A resident named Ann Knowles, curious to know what was taking place and what a pit shaft looked like, ventured too near, slipped and fell down the shaft. Rescuers who went to her assistance expected to find her dead or at least suffering from broken bones. To their profound astonishment they found her alive, suffering only from shock and a broken little finger. The reason given for her marvellous escape was that the crinoline dress of the period acted in the nature of a parachute and broke the force of the fall.

Before the opening of the Golborne mine the township was provided with a coal depot at the Smithies. The rail track from the Edge Green mine crossed the highway at a point below the Great Central Railway and proceeded to the Smithies parallel with the highway. The rails were laid on blocks of stone instead of the customary sleepers. The rail track was of the standard dimension and the trucks were of small design capable of carrying three to four tons. The trucks appear to have carried an identity plate. A few years ago, a local farmer engaged in moving a mound of earth came across a plate lettered *R. Evans & Co. No.I.* The track referred to is, at the time of writing, still discernible in a field close by the railway and near the road to Wigan. The trackway from Edge Green to the Bason has now been taken up as redundant.

Cotton Manufacture

In view of the importance of the cotton industry in Lancashire it is hardly surprising to hear of factories in Golborne. According to an early report the brothers Robert and Henry Worsley had a small factory in what became known as Factory Lane in 1833. The machinery was driven by a small engine of 14 h.p. Probably this was the first mill in Golborne to be driven by an engine: there had been other mills, some dating back to the fourteenth century, but they were operated by wind or water power and were used for grinding corn. On a map of 1744, the estate called The Mill House is mentioned, and we are informed that at one time John Peters occupied the Upper Mill, and Hugh Banks the Lower Mill. This Lower Mill was, no doubt, the Corn Mill in Mill Lane. Presumably the Upper Mill would be the one in Barn Lane now referred to by the name Blacking Mill. We have not found any evidence to support the story that at this mill shoe blacking was made. It was in fact a small weaving shed. Next to it, Mr William Mather built his jam factory.

In the earliest census returns is a note to the effect that "there are fustian weavers in the locality." Edward Crouchley was named as "one who had received an apprentice weaver in 1787." It is quite possible that fustian weaving was carried on at the Upper Mill.

We pass now to 1839 when the Brewis family built and equipped the Parkside Mill near the brook in Bridge Street. Evidently the management was in time controlled by John Brewis who, being an optimist so far as cotton spinning was concerned, built a larger and more elaborate mill in 1850. He was evidently an astute and far-seeing man capable of making a fortune in buying cotton alone. He built blocks of property for the workpeople - the Ten Row and School Street - and a school for half-timers. He is said to have erected a small gas plant for lighting the factory; this may have provided the idea of illuminating the township with coal gas which was, incidentally, introduced by a Mr Lawson in 1855.

A few years ago, a former Golborne resident then about eighty years of age, gave me a brief account of the prevailing conditions among young people who worked under the half-time system which he himself had experienced. He said "I was eight years old when I went to work at Brewis's New Mill in 1860. The time worked was from six in the morning, with half an hour for breakfast, until half-past twelve. One hour was allowed for dinner. In the afternoon we commenced at one-thirty until six in the evening, and on Saturdays we worked until two o'clock. My wage was one and threepence a week. I also remember the old corn mill in Mill Lane, but the Mill House and the Mill were then falling into ruin."

Mr Brewis died comparatively young in 1886 aged 63 years. Eventually the Parkside Mills were acquired by Messrs Brown & Nephew and, owing to the depression in the industry and trade fluctuations, they had wavering success. Finally the mills were closed and offered for sale. No purchasers were forthcoming until the First World War when the engines and machinery were sold. The buildings remained empty until an enterprising industrialist, Mr Harrison Benn, foresaw possibilities in the manufacture of viscose products. He bought the factories and formed a company under the namd of *Harbens* a combination of his names. He did not live to see the fulfilment of his ambition, and the business passed to new management. Several processing difficulties had to be overcome, but afterwards the new company entered a period of success, and now employs upwards of two thousand persons.

A factory in Harvey Lane known as the Co-op, was built for spinning and weaving. However, owing to insufficient capital, most of which had been provided from local sources, the promoters were unable to equip it with the full complement of machinery, and the rooms stood empty for a time. For a while one was occupied by the Wesleyan Methodists before they built a chapel and school in Heath Street.

In 1870 Joseph Howard installed some throstle spinning machinery. The man who has given the account of the conditions of the half-timers was then about eighteen years of age and was offered the job of Inside Manager of the Mill by Mr Howard. He accepted and continued working there until the closing down of the factory. The enterprise appears to have encountered numerous difficulties from its inception, and achieved only limited success. After a while the mill was taken over by Messrs Rothwells, cocoa and chocolate manufacturers. They made numerous alterations and additions to the buildings, and for several years the industry added materially to the welfare of the township. These premises were sold in 1931 to be used by Littlewoods for warehousing and by Davies and Twiss for milling.

Wallpaper Manufacture

The wallpaper, staining and varnishing business developed in Golborne about 1850. It was originally promoted by Mr William Mitchell who came from Manchester to reside in the district. Various stories are associated with the origin of the business, but the reliability of some of these is doubtful. As a young man Mr Mitchell had a flair for paper staining, marbling and the production of attractively designed wallpapers. He is said to have had a small business in Manchester but, owing to replanning within the city, his premises had to be demolished. While searching for a new site he came to Golborne and ultimately occupied some vacant property in Legh Street. He became associated with a young Liverpool business man, Mr Arnott, whose financial standing proved to be the substantial basis for a joint partnership. So an agreement was entered upon and after various difficulties had been overcome, the enterprise known as Mitchell & Arnott developed and prospered. At one period, owing to the growth of business a vacant room in the Co-operative factory formed temporary premises preparatory to the building of the Brookside Mill.

In those early days, warehousing and transport difficulties were common. Most of the manufactured products had to be sent by hand-cart or other means to the existing warehouse at Parkside. It was not until 1873 or thereabouts that a warehouse was built in the township in connection with the L.N.W.Railway. In spite of such difficulties the wallpaper concern prospered. The principal partners became keenly interested in local affairs and local government, Mr Mitchell, as a resident in the township, was particularly interested. He became chairman of the Council, a Justice of the Peace, and member of the County Council, and was keenly interested in religious and educational matters. Mr Arnott resided at Lowton. He also was promoted to the Bench and became a member of the County Council.

Unfortunately, in 1886, the Brookside Mill was destroyed by fire. The buildings were later restored and enlarged and ultimately the concern became merged in The Wallpaper Manufacturers Ltd. Among the relatives of the family who became connected with the paper-staining business was one who distinguished himself as a mechanic. He had a wonderful capacity for designing contrivances to expedite the process of staining and varnishing, and is reputed to have been the inventor of a roller, the first of its kind designed to impress varnish successfully on the printed papers in one operation.

Another well-known Lancashire firm who make a speciality of incorporating nursery rhymes on specially designed papers, as well as making sanitary wallpapers, are said to have sent valuable orders worth thousands of pounds to the Brookside Mill to be treated by this particular varnishing process. Later, when the wallpaper combine decided to close the Brookside Mill, this particular machine was transferred to the London branch of another well-known firm of wallpaper manufacturers.

Engineering

Success, like character, is not acquired by dreaming, it must be forged into being. Many have neglected opportunities and rejected the offers of fortune, being afraid of work or of the shock of contest. But though they decline the toil of climbing, they willingly "enjoy what they dare not seize" - so writes Dr. Johnson. Some we know, who, at the commencement of their careers, peddled their wares in this township,never expecting to earn a nation-wide reputation, but lived to found big businesses. Some as youths commenced with a mere pittance, persevered, sacrificed, and became employers. Wherever success has been attained it has been due to the determination and tenacity of the individual who, although "baffled, determined to fight better."

The Naylor Bros. are examples of such perseverance and initiative. This engineering firm was started by Charles and Joseph Naylor in 1894 as a small private company in unpretentious premises in Silcock Street. On the slender foundation of seventy pounds for capital, a now flourishing company has grown up. As one traveller said to another: "How do you find business?" "I go and look for it" was the reply. So it was with these people; they looked for work. They made gates, palisades for public buildings and private property, builder's ironwork, and undertook any other work that could be found. They worked very long hours and drew 25/- per week for wages. Any surplus was used to buy tools. After a few difficult years, the turning point in the business came with the first substantial order secured in London. This was obtained by travelling on the night excursion train, arranging the business during the day, using the midnight train home, and then working on the material next day in the shop. Such was the accepted order; hard work, long hours, and satisfied customers. This first substantial order was, as one partner declared, the open sesame to more business both in the capital and the provinces.

Now (1955) after well over half a century of progress the company has over seven hundred employees and is occupied with more extensive business, making colliery equipment of all kinds such as coal-washing machinery, steel haulage cages, elevators, skip hoists, transporters as supplied to leading modern power stations and gas works. All such business has meant not only designing and sending the machinery to places such as France, Turkey, India and other parts of the world, but representatives have also gone there to see the work correctly carried out. The enterprise continues to develop and is a valuable asset to other local industries.

The Golborne Gas Company 1855

It is quite evident that among our predecessors a century ago there were a few who were captivated by the idea of reducing the minor discomforts of life. Petroleum was used for lighting in 1847 and by 1855 the safety match was popular.

A local benefactor was Mr Lawson who, in 1855, erected in Golborne a small gas works. He had no parliamentary powers, and so progress was restricted. The works proved incapable of illuminating the growing town. Twelve years later in 1867, several prominent local gentlemen realising the need for better lighting and knowing that Mr Lawson had not the necessary capital to extend the enterprise approached him with a view to purchase and bought the works for £850. They then formed themselves into a limited company with a capital of £10,000.

The Memorandum of Association stated the object of the agreement which was to purchase the small works then existing. The subscribers were John Brewis, WilliamTravers, John Unsworth, Rev. C. T. Quirk, John Fearns, James Lawton, S. Shepherd, William Crowther and John Howard. Earlier, in 1861, the Leigh District Gas Co. having applied to Parliament to be incorporated as a statutory body included Golborne, along with other places, to be supplied with gas. The Leigh Company, however, never exercised the powers they were granted. At the hearing of evidence which ensued later it was revealed that the Chairman of the Golborne Company and the Chairman of the Leigh Company had held a friendly conference. The Leigh Chairman had definitely assured the Golborne Chairman that Leigh had no intention of supplying Golborne with Gas. Furthermore, they were willing to assist the Golborne Company and advise them how they could best supply the township themselves. They were prepared to lend their engineer, Mr Timmins, with this object in view. This arrangement, however, did not last.

When an announcement appeared in the Gazette in 1901 stating that the Golborne Company were on the point of asking Parliament to be placed on a statutory basis, trouble commenced. Leigh not only decided to exercise their latent powers, they also started to lay a gas main. Previously they had lain a ten inch main to Pennington where the pipe capacity was reduced to seven inches. Proceeding as far as Knott's Mill, almost on the Lowton boundary, the main had been reduced to five inches. The line was then extended to Lowton St. Mary's in a four inch pipe, and continued from a place below St. Mary's bridge to Lane Head in a three inch pipe.

The aim appears to have been to supply Lowton and to continue to the boundary at Lowton Junction. The obvious place from which the pipe line would proceed to supply Golborne would be Lane Head via Church Lane and Lowton Road. It may seem an amazing statement to make, but according to evidence given at the enquiry, the junction main destined to proceed to Golborne was to be increased to a six inch main, and again to a nine inch, and this was to be continued along Church Street. Apparently another obstacle had to be surmounted: the nine inch pipe was to be reduced to six inches, but having crossed the railway bridge, it was designed to continue as a nine inch main.

The Leigh people were all out to establish themselves in Golborne and were determined to oppose the local company's application. In this attempt they were assisted by the Urban District Council who also had lodged an objection, in spite of the fact that the Council had been given the option of purchasing the entire Golborne company's plant on behalf of the township. They had turned the offer down.

The litigation which commenced on May 9, 1901, in the Commons continued in the Lords where it terminated on August 9, 190l. Eminent counsel had been engaged by both parties, and the nominee for the

Golborne Council was their Chairman who gave evidence on behalf, and in support, of the Leigh proposal. Several searching questions were asked and one put to the Golborne Chairman during the examination was: "Have you purchased a ground rent of about four pounds a year to enable you to qualify for appointment on the Council?" It appears to be a somewhat tendentious query, and the inference, whatever it was, must have been best known to the questioner. The result of the litigation was a complete victory for the Golborne company who appear to have celebrated their success in a kind of triumphal entry into the township.

It is evident that the township could have owned its own gas supply and the profits accruing there from might have contributed substantially toward the rates for many years. Later, the company was re-constituted and the first directors were Fred Silcock, William Travers, John Yates, Richard Barker, Thomas Southern, Alfred Caunce and Thomas Silcock. ·

Until about 1950 Golborne was served from the Gas Works in John Street. Then St. Helens Corporation became responsible for the supply.

Water Supply

In earlier days before a piped water supply was available or even contemplated, the township depended principally on wells and springs. The picturesque windlass and oak bucket were the order of the day. Usually the well was enclosed, and in some instances the precaution of keeping it under lock and key was adopted. Where a public water supply was available the letter W was painted on a nearby house or wall. One such place which retains its former designation was Holt's Well which supplied the few nearby dwellings. From the Abram side the ground rose to the well, forming a brow. Residents referred to Holt's Well Brow in the briefest possible manner; they dropped the Holt and retained the S which was added to well - so the name remains to this day in the vernacular Swell Brow.

There were numerous draw wells and nearby all the farms had pumps, some being installed in the house. Some farms had reserve tanks and other supplies were collected in rainwater butts. Old marl pits provided supplies for cattle, and the brook (before wholesale pollution took place) was an additional source of supply for livestock on near-by meadows. For hygienic reasons these former sources have now been deemed unsuitable except in a few isolated instances. There are abundant underground supplies in the district and probably for this reason the Parish Council in earlier days made insufficient effort to provide a good supply, preferring to buy water from the Ince Waterworks and from an installation set up on land adjacent to Lowton Road. Advantages may have accrued immediately, but the supply of 1875 has not kept pace with industrial and domestic requirements. The problem of an adequate supply continues to increase.

Consumption in Golborne in 1953 was 240,000 gallons daily and in Lowton 120,000 gallons. Culcheth depends on the Warrington Corporation. The principal supply for Golborne is designated hard. Although the Urban District Council have made various attempts to develop a water softening process there appear to be certain difficulties which have yet to be overcome. The need for a good supply of water increases. Owners of attested milk-producing herds will no longer be permitted to use the old sources of supply, and piped water will be as necessary for tuberculin free cows as it is for human beings. This problem is not just local since we have observed how acutely other townships can be affected in times of even temporary drought.

A group of Golborne children inspecting storm damage about 1912.

Chapter V
Transport
Roads

Any attempt to give a detailed description of the roads of the township can only be a partial success unless consideration is given to roads in general. Volumes have already been written about these, so only a few salient features will be presented here.

The Romans made roads which lasted many years, but between the fifth and the seventeenth century not a single road was deliberately planned or constructed.

An attempt was made in 1285 by the Statute of Winchester to improve conditions but the provisions were not generally enforced. When the responsibility devolved on the lord of the manor he usually succeeded in passing it on to the occupier of the land adjoining the highway. He, in turn, evaded it as much as possible.

The Church, very creditably, undertook road maintenance and the repair of bridges. Each parish was also responsible for road maintenance and had the duty of appointing a person known as the Surveyor of Highways. It was the usual procedure at the Vestry Meeting for four substantial householders to nominate the Surveyor of Highways for the year in Easter week. He might not know anything about road repair yet he had to accept; if he refused he was liable to a fine of two pounds.

In the time of the Tudors these tracks which served as roads were not properly maintained and lacked boundaries of any kind. As one track became worn down, another appeared by its side and the roadway became upwards of a hundred yards wide. Sloughs and ruts were common.

A statutory enactment in 1555 ordered "that householders should bring shovels, baskets and carts and assemble at a stated place to effect road repair." This continued until 1800 as the following excerpt from *The Antiquities of Lancashire and Cheshire* illustrates:-

*At a certain time the Surveyor of Highways gave
the parish clerk notice for a day's work on the
highways. On Sunday next, the Clerk rushing out of
Church at the close of service in the afternoon
cries - "O Yez! O Yez! - this is to give notice
that the inhabitants of Church Coppenhall are
requested to meet at Cross Green on Wednesday
morning at eight o'clock with picks and shovels,
to repair the highways. God save the King!"*

These observations apply to roads in general; interest develops as we peruse the subject as it relates more closely to the township.

In his *Observations of Lancashire and Cheshire*, Adam Watkin, approaching from Cheshire, wrote thus:-

*We now enter Lancashire, the County of Industry.
For many ages, to the middle of the eighteenth
century, a causeway about two feet broad, paved
with pebbles was all that man and beast could travel
upon through Lancashire and Cheshire. The causeway
was guarded with posts to keep carts off, and the open
parts of the road were generally impassable in
winter for mire and deep ruts. In winter no coach
durst venture through. The narrow causeway was the
source of vexation. Travellers would meet on it,
and as there was no suitable place where they
could pass, neither party would give way. Each one
did his best to push the other on the open road, usually
into a quagmire from which it was difficult to
extricate man or beast.*

The Leigh road was no better "having great ruts and hollows deep enough to bury a sheep." Arthur Young who travelled extensively on our main highway described it as "most execrably vile, with ruts four feet deep." The Wigan to Altrincham road was worse, and he advises travellers "to avoid the road as they would the Divill, for a thousand to one they would break their necks." John Wesley, whom we may regard as a veteran traveller, travelled thousands of miles in the course of his mission and "paid more tolls than any man who ever bestrode a beast." In his Journal he writes "April 3, 1772, I set out for Wigan, but before we came to Ashton I was glad to use my own feet and leave the poor horses to drag the chaise as best they could." Earlier, Miss Celia Fiennes had in 1698 travelled our main highway and noted at Wigan "mostly lanes and some hollow wayes, and some pretty deep stony way so forced us up on the high Causey many times ..., I was 5 hours going that 14 miles"... Again "I passed through abundance of villages, almost at the end of every mile, mostly along lanes. They have one good thing in this County Palatine that at the end of all cross ways, there are posts with the names of the great towns that it leads to."

The last excerpt reflects creditably on Lancashire people who had been prompt in carrying out their duties, for the statute which ordained "that direction posts or stones should be set up at all crossroads" had been enacted only one year previously.

The earliest known bridge in the county dates from 1364. It crossed the Mersey at Warrington. No longer need pack animals be unladen or ferried over, nor need travellers ford or swim across. The bridge was the gratuitous service provided by religious institutions. Travellers gladly contributed a monetary payment to "A certain Brother John the Hermit, licenced to perform divine office at the foot of the bridge and to receive gifts."

The government did little to make the roads sound, contenting itself with passing regulations concerning the carriages using them. Road users were prohibited from driving more than four horses together tandem fashion. It was an offence to drive two horses abreast or for a vehicle to carry more than one ton, as this was regarded as a public nuisance.

The tyre of the wheel was also a contentious subject. The use of one less than nine inches in breadth was not permissible. An offender was liable to a fine of five pounds, or one month in prison. Tyres, thirteen inches in breadth, were made at Brock Forge, Wigan, and tyres sixteen inches broad were recommended "as they would roll the road."

When the turnpike trusts operated, the first local instance of turnpike rioting occurred on the St. Helens to Ashton road, when the trust levied an increased toll charge and insisted on the use of the broad wheel. The trust could erect toll houses, toll gates, bars - also spiked bars - and weighing machines and could impound horses in excess of the prescribed number. Pike - (S)pike-men - were usually dressed in tall black hats, corduroy breeches and white stockings, but we have no information about their operating bars or gates within the township.

The nearest toll bar was at the entrance of Stone Cross Lane near the Newton road, and the toll house remains in habitable condition. The toll gate and posts, part of the barrier, were taken for scrap metal during the Second World War, although in good condition. The remaining gate and posts were saved from destruction by the shrewdness of the occupier of Lowton House Farm where they now serve as entrance gates. With the tolls collected some improvements were made to the roads. Various changes occurred in the resurfacing of the roads and the paivers were at work locally in 1710. Blue boulder stone was carted from the Sankey canal wharf at Winwick, two shillings a day being the local rate for man, horse and cart. The cost of the paved road was £3,000 per mile.

Administration Of Roads

Owing to the difficulty of obtaining precise information only a few deductions can be made about the administration of Golborne roads.

As we had no parish church until 1850, and as the vestry did not exist, the Surveyor of Roads would have been nominated by the parochial committee, subject to the approval of the ratepayers. Various decisions of the parochial committee appear to have been subject to the approval of the Rural Sanitary Authority of the Leigh Union.

The parochial committee, the Highways Board and most likely other committees met in schoolrooms, business offices and other places, for there was no recognised office for dealing with the affairs of the township until 1887 "when a meeting of the ratepayers was held on September 1 of that year to decide whether the consent of the vestry shall be given to the Overseers, with the consent of the Local Government Board, to provide an office for the transaction of the business of the parish by the purchasing of freehold property in Worsley Street." Consent was given and the property acquired. It is not improbable that many valuable documents have been misplaced owing to there not having previously been a central office.

The appointment of Highways Surveyor was for a period of one year only. Amongst the earliest recorded names is that of Richard Fearns. Combined with the office was that of the Inspector of Nuisances at a salary of two pounds a year.

Twenty years ofter this appointment, Mr C.S. Bennie was appointed Surveyor at a salary of £50 and he continued in office for ten years at the same salary. Mr Bennie served the district for thirty years and during his period of office all the main highways were reconstructed and were accounted second to none in the locality.

Byeways

A stranger entering the township by the Warrington to Wigan road in the late eighteen sixties might have seen the rebuilding of the bridge as he entered the Dale. The principal pillar was dated and the word Golburne implying boundary, was inscribed. From that point onward to the township, the road was known as Platt Lane, a name possibly derived from platt or plot of land.

Leading off Platt Lane was Colonel's Lane by the end of the wood, forming an approach to the park. Nearer the township was Cop Lane, which continued as Park Vue and finally Park Road. From Cop Lane, Sandy Lane and Barn Lane both connected with Harvey Lane and Bank Heath.

A distinctive feature of the area is the frequent reference to lanes although attempts have been made to modernise the term. From the lanes the various streets developed, and as occasion arose these were named with the surname or Christian name of prominent townspeople to give us John, Charles, Wilmot, Helen, Mitchell, Silcock, Wakefield and Turton streets.

Railways

When the Liverpool to Manchester passenger carrying railway, the first in the kingdom, was completed in 1830, it proved to be a great incentive towards the improvement of industries and also stimulated further developments in transport. The country at the time was served by a network of canals. Although the Duke of Bridgewater who made a canal from his collieries near Worsley to Manchester (1758-60) is acclaimed "the father of the canal system" we should not overlook the construction of the St. Helens and Sankey canal in 1756, described as "the first navigable inland canal in the Kingdom."

Conveyance of goods by waterway had its limitations. Cargoes had to be handled frequently and transport was still slow, though cheap as compared with the alternative transport by road. Canal transport was now due to be offset by a more expeditious method. The steam engine had arrived. The mania for making railways developed, and the Liverpool to Manchester railway helped to set the pace. No sooner had Stephenson completed one track than he was busy with another. The huge strata of rock at Edge Hill and the quaking bog of Chat Moss had failed to deter the engineers.

After the completion of the Liverpool to Manchester line, the Warrington to Newton Bridge line was constructed at a cost of £65,000 and opened in July of 1831. Then followed the line from Chapel Lane, Wigan, to Parkside in September 1832. This line connected with the main line at Parkside via Lowton Junction. Trains from Wigan and beyond destined for Manchester branched off at Lowton junction and continued along the cutting which formerly was known as the North Union Railway. This branch section came to be used whenever the Royal train stayed overnight in this part of the county.

Trains bound for Liverpool, Chester or the south were diverted to the other branch line and this route to Warrington proceeded by way of Earlestown Junction.

Trains from the south to Preston and the north came by Earlestown and Newton and proceeded by Lowton Junction. This route proved too roundabout and valuable time was lost so the Winwick Branch Line was planned constructed and opened in 1867. Starting in the Winwick district it proceeded direct to Golborne Dale were it connected with the former main line and so relieved the growing congestion at Earlestown and Newton. The railway through Golborne crossed Tanner's Lane by a level crossing and later again crossed the main highway to Wigan near the parish church. Part of the original highway is still to be seen there. Here, the short approach known as Railway Road was protected by gates. There was an old tavern which did service for the present Railway Hotel. The keeper of the gates was a Mr Ashcroft of a well known Golborne family who, as well as carrying out his duties as gate-keeper assisted his wife who acted as booking clerk. At that time the tickets showing destination and fare were made out by hand. The increasing flow of traffic and the slow and dangerous opening and closing of the gates led to the building of a bridge over the railway at this point.

In 1884 or thereabouts another line was planned alongside the existing line so that the trains from north to south could pass the slower moving traffic between Springs Branch and Golborne Dale. This necessitated closing the level crossing at Tanners Lane where a bridge was constructed to accommodate the additional lines. This extra service was known locally as the fast line. Charles Braddock was the contractor.

The facilities for warehousing for manufacturers and others for upwards of forty years were provided by a small stone-built warehouse erected at Parkside. Soon, not only was it too small, but it was inconvenient and could not cope with the expanding needs of the district. Golborne people petitioned the L.N.E.Ry.Co. for the erection of more suitable premises and a warehouse was built near the passenger station. The Parkside warehouse was closed and was taken down about 1900.

The original passenger station at Parkside also proved too inconvenient. Newton le Willows was much more suitable, so the former station was closed and converted into dwellings which are still in use.

It was also at Parkside that the first notable railway fatality occurred. The event and the occasion were memorable, and it is not surprising to hear various local people whose ancestors assisted in the making of the Newton, Parkside and Golborne section of the railway refer to the event. Mr Jonathan Worral for instance, the first station master at Parkside, was present at the opening ceremony in September 1830 of the Liverpool-Manchester railway, and saw the unfortunate accident which resulted in the death of Mr William Huskisson, M.P This gentleman, who had been prominent in promoting measures for the railway, descended from the train which had been halted to allow for replenishing the water supply for the engine - *The Rocket*. The statesman, who had previously had some difference of opinion with the Duke of Wellington, seeing him in one of the carriages, stepped forward to shake hands with him. He was unfortunately struck by *The Rocket* (which was then returning to the train) and seriously injured. Although Mr Huskisson was rushed away to a house as speedily as possible and every effort was made to save his life he died later in the day. A little below the site where the warehouse stood, in a recess in the wall, is a memorial tablet describing the event. Mr Christopher Naylor was another witness. He had helped to build the railway and frequently met George Stephenson. Being musically inclined, Mr Naylor joined the Old Leigh Band and played on several notable occasions including that of the Chartist demonstrations at Kersal Moor. When the Parkside Mill Band was formed, he became the conductor and also became choir-master at the church he attended. His son, also named Christopher, father of the founders of Messrs. Naylor Bros., was also one of the founders of the British Schools and Science classes.

Through the greater portion of his life Mr Abel Turton held the position of station master at Lowton Junction. He is credited with being the first to introduce the red rear light adopted by all trains. Whether he ever received any official recognition we have yet to learn. As a man he was of a kindly and courteous disposition and his loyalty to duty will long be remembered. A memorial in Bridge Street Methodist Church commemorates his work in the Sunday School and Church.

The London and North Eastern Railway, usually referred to as the Great Central, was planned to give additional service to the district. It was devised to connect Manchester with Liverpool by an alternative route. Its failure to do so is attributed to financial reasons. The service eventually connected St. Helens with Manchester as a branch line. It was completed in 1880 but is now rarely used as a passenger service. The nationalisation of the railways in 1948 is the latest development in their history.

Chapter VI
The Church

No church existed in Golborne before 1849. For several centuries Winwick was the recognised place of public worship for numerous townships within the Hundred. For the convenience of the inhabitants of Ashton, Newton and Culcheth there were chapelries supervised from Winwick where the rector and curates were in residence. The inhabitants of Golborne and Lowton had many difficulties to contend with. Transport facilities were negligible, roads were often impassable, especially in winter, and weather conditions and distance made it impossible for the aged and infirm to attend Winwick. The few who did attend from the several townships may well have conveyed their impressions to the interested adherents who were unable to attend.

Winwick was renowned for ministers of exceptional ability. The Rev.J. Rider in 1596 published a Latin dictionary, believed to be the first of its kind ever produced. The Rev. Charles Herle, M.A., a distinguished scholar of Presbyterian sympathies, was appointed to the living in 1626. He was a member of the Association of Divines and was appointed to licence books on divinity. Both in London and Lancashire he acquired fame aa a preacher and became a favourite in the Long Parliament. The list of exceptional men could be extended considerably, for Winwick has a remarkable literary history.

Charles Herle had been appointed to the living at Winwick by Sir Thomas Stanley. He was on intimate terms with William, the sixth Earl of Derby, and was tutor to his son James, afterwards known as the Martyr Earl. Rector Herle did not share the political view of his patron, as might have been expected, for his religious sympathy was on the side of dissent.

John Howe, later to become one of the most distinguished preachers in the country, was educated at Winwick Grammar School and was later ordained at Winwick by the Rev. Charles Herle. The historian, J.R. Green writes: "No English divine save Jeremy Taylor rivalled Howe as a preacher." Dr. Watts, who attended his services in Westminster Abbey, wrote an ode in his honour. Howe rose above the narrow and bigoted controversy which disfigured the period and it is said that the happiest years of his life were spent as minister at Great Torrington. He was appointed domestic chaplain to Cromwell and on one occasion preached for two hours at Whitehall. After the Restoration, he suffered, along with hundreds of other ministers, from the intolerance of the Act of Uniformity. Several ministers in the immediate neighbourhood among the many who were deprived of their livings may be mentioned, namely: Rev.J. Wood of Ashton-in-Makerfield, Rev. J. Wright, M.A. of Billinge, Rev. Robert Yates, Rector of Warrington, Rev. C. Hotham, Rector of Wigan and the Rev. Thomas Risley, of Warrington. It is a memory worthy of preserving that among our predecessors in those far away days, there were men whom the spoils of office did not attract and who placed their honour first.

However, in spite of the attraction of brilliant ministers at Winwick, it is not surprising that some zealous parishioners of Golborne, faced with difficulties of transport, determined to improve conditions. In 1650 when a commission dealing with church affairs was in session at Wigan, they had before them this petition:-

> Wee present, that the towne of Gouldburne lyeth within
> the parish of Winwick - the Tythe thereof is worth
> by the yeare, Thirty ffyve pounds which is part of the
> sum of ffower hundred and forty five pounds and two
> shillings and has been paid and gathered for the use
> of Mr Charles Herle pson of Winwicke who supplyes
> the Cure there, and wee think fitt, that the inhabitants
> of Gouldburne shall joyne with Lowton for the building
> of a Chapel at the Stone Cross in Lowton and be part
> of that parish for their ease and good...

The commission was impressed with the reasonableness of the request and agreed that a chapelry should be built, but, as with many other good intentions, matters were allowed to drift and no active measures were taken to implement the request. Eighty years passed by. The promoters of the scheme passed on and the opportunity which otherwise might have altered the situation appreciably so far as Golborne was concerned was missed. Eventually in 1731 The Lowton Chapel Agreement was concluded and following this in 1733 a chapel was built at Lowton and consecrated by the

Bishop of Chester in October of the same year. The Agreement remained for well over a hundred years and its continuance may well account for the absence of many records and decisions dealing with affairs strictly relating to Golborne. Most matters, and there were many, affecting the welfare of the township came within the purview of the church. No doubt these were dealt with at Lowton though the registers for the period were kept at Winwick.

In 1841, an Act was passed for dividing the Rectory of Winwick. Croft, Ashton, Newton, Lowton, Culcheth, Golborne and Haydock became separate ecclesiastical districts, the tithe being transferred from the rector of Winwick to the newly made rectors. Provision was made that Golborne and Haydock should be separated only when the population had reached two thousand and a church capable of seating six hundred had been provided. Nearly ten years after the passing of this act Golborne parish church was built.

The Stone Cross at Lowton

When in 1650, the Golborne petitioners had requested the church commissioners for a chapel to serve the common interests of Lowton and Golborne they had stated that the appropriate place for one was at the Stone Cross at Lowton. Almost three hundred years have passed by and we now see that Lowton along with some other townships, has been joined with Golborne for administrative purposes in local governnment and so we are still indirectly associated with this one-time popular landmark, the Stone Cross.

Whether it was a site cross, a direction cross, a preaching cross or mourners' cross, also known as a resting cross, no one appears to know. The only information is that it was of stone, but nothing is recorded about its shape, size or the direction in which the arms pointed. One cannot understand the senseless exhibition of vandalism which is ever ready to destroy all such reminders of a past age. An antiquarian of repute who resided in the township in 1837 recorded: "I have learned that the land where the Cross stood is about to be enclosed, and that five lime trees are planted on the land in the shape of a cross."

No description is given of the position of this land. Among the oldest residents are those who claim to have seen the lime trees on the un-enclosed land referred to as the stone croft. A legal friend gave me an extract from a deed in his possession dated 3 June 1783, but no plan is attached to it. The extract reads:

All that tenement and two orchards being all together and containing half an acre of land lying North-West of Lowton Chapel and North of the Stone Cross also three separate closes and parcels of ground hereinafter mentioned, the Great Barnfield containing three acres lying East of the said tenement and contiguous to the Little Barnfield: Little Barnfield containing two acres being North of Great Barnfield and contiguous thereto and The Old Roman's Meadow containing three acres lying East and contiguous to Little Barnfield...now in the tenure of Henry Coobs.

Having examined the tithe map dated 1837, I have found many of the names as well as the field numbers almost illegible but an attached schedule refers to upwards of a score of Barnfields. There are two Barnfields lying north-west of Lowton Chapel and also north of the presumed site of the Cross, one being slightly over three acres in extent and the other slightly short of two acres. These are in proximity to the Old Roman Meadow.

The tithe map states Woman's Meadow. The extract from the deed states Roman's Meadow. The particulars on the tithe map and schedule are hand written. An error seems to have been made in the copying, otherwise the data is substantially correct and agrees with the position of the lime trees on the unenclosed land almost opposite St. Luke's Church. The Old Woman's field was a portion of land behind the Old Rectory and between that and Laurel House. The name of Henry Coobs is not mentioned.

Nonconformity

Although Roman Catholicism survived in south-west Lancashire Puritanism also established itself, James I declared in May 1618: "In our progress through Lancashire we find two sets of people wherewith the county is infested, we mean Papists and Puritans." Though attempts were made to suppress both, the remarkable thing is that men reverenced their conscience more than their king and were prepared to make sacrifice, whether it was loss of home, or possessions, or even life itself, rather than give up their beliefs. In 1584, Rev. Fr. James Bell had been condemned according to statute, for saying mass in Golborne "upon St. John's day Christmas last." Mr Bell was a native of Orford near Warrington, educated Oxford, and along with Rev.J. Finch of Eccleston was tried at Lancaster "both being accused of high treason. They refused to take the oath and suffered at Lancaster the following April." For people who know little or nothing about religious persecution "suffering at Lancaster" was a horrible event, and that is a mild way of stating a disagreeable fact.

After the Revolution of 1688, religious toleration was allowed to all except Roman Catholics and Unitarians. Preaching licences were introduced, applicants appealing the court for permission to preach in a dwelling. The following licence was issued on 21 July 1690:

These are to certify whom it may concern that the
house of Peter Gaskill of Burtonwood of the County
now certified to the Court for a meeting place for
a congregation of Protestants dissenting from the
Church of England for the exercise of their worship
in it (pursuant to a late Act of Parliament) given
under my hand in open Court, recorded at the Quarter
Sessions,
Given under my hand George Kenyon, Clerk of the Peace.

Between the years 1811 and 1825 William Alexander an itinerant preacher, travelled between Prescot and Leigh with the intention of founding a Society of Independents (Congregationalists) in both places. In his travels he occasionally called at Newton and Edge Green both places being mentioned in his notes. In his visit to Newton he describes sending several boys to announce that he would be preaching immediately at the Cross which in those days stood directly opposite the front entrance of St. Peter's church near the present remains of the stocks. "When I commenced," he writes, "I was forcibly pulled down from the steps of the Cross by the Constable."

Describing his visit to Edge Green he continues: "The People here are notoriously wicked and beastly intemperate and the place is the scene of many fights...a notable Prizefighter dwells among them!" The mission of

Mr Alexander soon began to have effect, however. There were glimmerings of hope, and instead of oaths and curses, songs of praise could be heard ascending from the mine." This incidentally is the first intimation of coal mining in the district. Mr Alexander's work was beginning to take a practical turn. In Golborne in 1828 a small company of people began to hold preaching services in the granary of Jane Pierpoint's farm at the end of Park Road. Both Mrs Pierpoint and her son Joseph encouraged and supported the movement and later were prominent in providing the first place for public worship in the township. This was in Tanner's Lane and was used as a meeting place and Sunday School.

Other Societies came into being later with the Methodists at Edge Green, where a community was established with a small chapel on the green a short distance from the highway. This movement received substantial support from Messrs. Evans and other members of the mining industry. The chapel soon became too small for the Society and was later turned into a day school. The members of the cause established themselves in the present buildings. A similar Society commenced in Golborne, bearing the name Primitive - a designation which appears to have originated because of some difference of opinion more about methods than doctrine. The Primitive Methodist Society commenced in a small cottage in Mill Street and later, in 1847, established itself in Bridge Street. The Independent Methodists known as Free Gospellers started in the same year. The Wesleyan Methodists began as a Society in a disused room in the Co-operative factory and later established themselves in Heath Street with a chapel and Sunday school.

The Baptist Society developed later and opened a place of worship in Charles Street in 1894. Meanwhile a number of families, many of them of Welsh extraction, were beginning to move into the township and they decided to build with the result that we had both a Welsh Congregational and Welsh Methodist Church. Both buildings have proved to be redundant and have been taken over for other purposes. The Roman Catholic church was built in 1927.

Chantries

The story affecting the religious aspirations of inhabitants both within the parish and the Hundred would not be complete without mentioning chantries. There is no proof of any such places in Golborne. Richard, Prior of Nostel, gave Sir Robert Banastre licence to have a chantry at Rokedene in a chapel there within the parish of Winwick. Whether the few people who lived at Golborne in past days were sufficiently devout to take advantage of this we cannot say.

This chantry, described as the chantry chapel of Newton stood, according to Mr Beamont, "nearby where John Stirrup erected a school, somewhere in Golborne Hollows." Such places were sometimes built by private persons on their own property and located in quiet situations remote from the mother church, which was, at certain times of the year, almost inaccessible to the aged and infirm, owing to bad roads and inclement weather.

It is said "that the original intention of founding such places was that they were simply...for private prayer." Within Winwick Church itself a chantry was founded by Sir Gilbert de Haydock in 1330. In the Historical Society's Review Mr Farrar refers to an Inquiry held on 4 February 1328, "when a Commission advised the King to give consent to Sir Gilbert as Haydock to assign seven messuages, seven tofts, thirty-eight acres and three roods of land in Newton to a Chaplain to celebrate divine service in the Chapel of Holy Trinity at Wynquyk for the soul of Gilbert and for the souls of his father and mother and all faithfull departed."

Private chapels were common among the wealthy in the fifteenth century and usually such families maintained a chaplain. These private chapels were principally for the gathering together of the family for prayer and devotion and not for the celebration of the ordinances of the Church. Within a radius of three miles of the township set; such chapels are to be found connected with some of the halls and other notable houses. Many of them have since been turned to other uses.

After the suppression of the monasteries and the taking of their wealth, the monarch turned to the chantries, collegiate churches, hospitals and guilds. The government considered the property of these foundations to be the property of the king who was ready to secularise it for his own purposes. "Principles of justice and equity were set aside. Legal security was not acknowledged. The rights of property were unrecognised and disregarded."

81

This confiscation of church property by the Tudor monarchs deprived the poor of a source of relief in times of distress. The result was that later, for their support, poor rates had to be levied on land, houses and other property.

Schools and Schoolmasters

The preamble of the act ordering the dissolution of the chantries alluded to the erection of grammar schools. It is interesting to note that Gowther Legh, son of Sir Peter Legh, knight and priest, had anticipated this and had already contemplated the erection of a school at Winwick. In his will, made in 1546, a few years before the act, he donated certain sums of money to a few beneficiaries "for sending their sons to school." Gowther Legh died 1553 having provided for the foundation and endowment of a grammer school at Winwick. One Henry Johnson, a former curate and priest, released from his vows of celibacy, married and became the first schoolmaster there. Reference is made to him in the inscription on the church wall. A further inscription on the school wall states:

This howse was builte by Sir Peter Legh -
knight - upon his own charges in the yere
of our Lord to be a schoole hous for ever for
the free schoole at Winwicke founded by
Gualter Legh, Esquire, great uncle of the
said Sir Peter Legh, which Gualter gave ten
pounds of yerly rent for the perpetual
maintenance of the said school, and the
said Sir Peter hath augmented the same
with ten pounds per annum more, which he
hath assured to be yearlye payde to the same
free schoole for ever, for his zeal of
God's glory and his Love to the parish of
WinWick, and common good of the countrey.

In pre-Reformation days the village school was usually held in the church porch. This extract from the Charity Commissioner's Report describing Bankes' Charity shows how the school developed. "It is understood that J. Bankes who was schoolmaster in 1775 gave £3 yearly rent to buy books for the use of children who would attend the day school in Winwick churchyard." The Winwick school had a notable reputation, and another diarist states that "multitudes were almost annually sent to the University." Several eminent persons were educated there, and one scholar from Lowton, Richard Mather, at the early age of seventeen was recommended to Toxteth Grammar School where he was appointed master. We have not been able to gather any information relating to the education of Golborne children during this period, although it is possible that some families may have had a private tutor. At least one family on the Golborne boundary had one, for Roger Lowe mentions in his diary: "August 18,1675. About ten of the clocke dyed Mr Coe. He was schoole master there to Mr Sorrocoldes child and...Mr Sorrocolde reposed great trust in tutoring of his sonne and left £10 per annum and his diet until his son came of age."

The commencement of a school in Golborne itself was first undertaken in 1791, when Mr Wilmot Street, Mr Samuel Street and eleven others "being desirous of establishing a school in the township for the instructing the children in reading and writing and in other useful learning" built a school and dwelling house for the master in Golborne. An endowment of £120 was provided, bearing interest at 5% per annum. The school was part of the house and had a yard and garden attached. It was provided that a specified number of poor children of the township should be taught free of expense, and out of the interest the schoolmaster was to keep the premises in good repair. The master had to be a person practising the principles of the church of England and was to be free to take other scholars at a charge.

By 1855 the school buildings had become extremely dilapidated and the number of scholars reduced to six. Serious irregularities concerning the master being brought to light, the trustees dismissed him and appealed to the education authorities for assistance in restoring the building. The authorities appear to have agreed provisionally and recommended that a new school be built on a different site. Thomas Legh, esq., Lord of the Manor, is said to have granted to the rector and churchwardens of Golborne and their successors "a piece of land for this purpose to be in union with the National Society" in 1856. Under the authority of the Charity Commissioners dated March 24, 1857, the trustees applied to the County Court for an order for the sale of the old school and for the application of the proceeds towards the erection of the new school on the site recently granted. At a court held in Leigh on May 2, 1857, Mr Hulton the County

Court Judge heard arguments for and against the proposed order, six of the trustees opposing it on the grounds   "that it would hand over to a purely Church of England body school and endowment which were not in their origin so appropriated and that it compelled them to divest themselves of their property and hand it over to other trustees." After taking time for consideration, the judge refused the application. At the instance of the Charity Commissioners the case was re-heard and again the judge delivered a similar decision based on the application alone. Regardless of the opinion of the education authorities the school building was repaired, and by 1867 there were 45 boys on the books. But in 1868 the building was abandoned and the house let for a weekly rent of 2/6d.

The rector and others thereupon set about obtaining funds for a new school and applied to the Charity Commissioners for a scheme on the lines of that requested in 1857. The Commissioners felt bound to insist on the insertion in the trust deed of a conscience clause in accordance with Lord Cranworth's Act passed in 1860. The rector and trustees declined to agree so nothing was done. However, in 1870 a school was built and maintained by Mr John Brewis for the benefit of the half-timers, the children who worked in the cotton factory.

Owing to prevailing and increasing differences between Anglicans and Nonconformists, a few of the principal Non-conformists in the township decided to build and in 1877-8 the British School was erected opposite the present Congregational Church. The first school managers were Wm. Mitchell J.P., Christopher Naylor, T. Twist, Roger Yates, George Unsworth and W.R. Mitchell. Mr Ralph Douglas was appointed first master, a service to which he devoted himself assiduously. Unfortunately, his zeal exceeded his strength and having given unsparingly of his best he passed on after ten years of strenuous service. His activities were not confined to teaching for he was one of the promoters of the Golborne Mechanics institute and first secretary of the Mutual Improvment Society founded in 1878.

Mr T.J. Gilmour succeeded him as schoolmaster. He, too, was a man of progressive ideas and genial disposition who took an active interest in the welfare of his scholars and was ideally equipped for his work. His influence for good remains with many of us as a happy memory. In the top classes there were usually a number of book prizes to be gained for "good conduct and industry" and sometimes a silver medal inscribed "First."

Reflecting on those early years now that judgment is more mature and unbiased one can unhesitatingly say that both headmasters and staff did their best to produce good results from the material parents provided, some of which was of a rather disappointing nature. In addition to school work Mr Gilmour was interested in social welfare and for a time officiated as organist at the Church of the Founders.

Subsequently, owing to educational and administrative changes and the increased number of scholars in the limited accommodation, such schools were taken over as Provided schools.

Further reorganisation in 1912 resulted in the establishment of the new and commodious Council Schools where keen disciplinarian, Mr William V. Heyworth took charge up to the time of his retirement in 1950.

It may be noticed that no mention is made in the report of the commissioners of the names of the schoolmasters apart from that of Mr Isaac Taylor. A few names have been given to me but, lacking means of corroboration, I have refrained from mentioning them. Possibly Mr Taylor's most distinguishing feature was his beautiful copperplate writing, an outstanding success, taught to so many of his pupils. Afterwards, there followed Mr R. Wolacott; succeeding him Mr John Sourse and later Mr Thomas Southern. Mr Smith for a long period was Head of the half- timers school. For the Roman Catholics the All Saints School was founded in 1896.

Charities

In dealing with Golborne's schools, reference has already been made to one of the charities - that of Mr Wilmot Street. Details of other charities are given by the commission appointed to enquire into the charities of the parish of Winwick in their report of the proceedings held on 22 and 24 February and 26 April, 1900. This extensive document of over ninety pages describes in detail the various endowments which gave contributions to the hospitals, convalescent homes and nursing societies, financial assistance to the needy, blankets to the poor, Bibles to children and aid to schools and chapels. The charities it enumerates relate to the township of Winwick with Hulme, Newchurch, Middleton with Arbury, Haydock, Kenyon, Croft, Newton-in-Makerfield, Lowton and Golborne.

The charities relating to Golborne are those of Wilmot Street, Leadbeater, the Mather and Hooper's Charity and Miss Frances Moon's Charity. By her will in 1888, Miss Moon bequeathed £1,000 free of legacy duty to the rector and churchwardens of Golborne "for the sick and aged poor of Golborne." Owing to a failure of the assets, the bequest was reduced to about £400 which lay, in the bank unused until 1897. Then, at the instance of the Charity Commissioners, the churchwardens, who pleaded ignorance of the existence of the charity, invested the accumulated fund (£411.13.9d) in consols. There is now a yearly distribution from this charity. The Mather and Hooper Charities are for small amounts only. The Wilmot Street Charity dates back to 1791, and relates to the establishment of a school for children of the parish.

The deed whereby Leadbeater's Charity was founded has been lost. William Leadbeater in his will of 12 March 1685 stated that he had in his possession certain properties in Lowton and Golborne which he had already settled so that "a yearly profit might be paid to the poor living in Golborne and Lowton equally between them for ever." He further directed "that a large stone should be laid on his burial place and inscribed so that people might read and know how he had left his estate to the poor of Lowton and Golborne." A substantial amount of over £1,500 accrued from royalties and farm rents and was invested in console. Some land in Heath Street and Bank Street was also leased for building purposes and continues to bring in a yearly income. The proceeds from a farm house and buildings in Lowton are still administered by persons appointed to deal with the charity, new appointments being made periodically. It is now argued that as there are no poor people in either township the need to make disbursements no longer exists and the work of the charity is now being met from the National Exchequer. A committee has been appointed to inquire into the law relating to charitable trusts, and its terms of reference are:

> To consider and report on the changes in the law and practice (except as regards taxation) relating to charitable trusts in England and Wales, which would be necessary to enable the maximum benefit to the community to be derived from them.

It is not unreasonable to assume that the charity might provide some amenities for the township if its funds are no longer needed for their original purposes.

Dora Greenwell: Devotional Writer

Dora Greenwell was the daughter of William Thomas Greenwell, a country squire, a Justice of the Peace and Deputy Lieutenant for his county. "She was born December 6, 1821 at Greenwell Ford, near Lanchester, County Durham. Greenwell Ford has been the family residence for some three centuries and has been described as charming being somewhat secluded in a woodland setting through which a winding stream makes its way to the Weir two miles from Durham. The poetess later in life wrote of "this sweet stream the haunt of solitary hern and shy kingfisher."

Her father, of kindly disposition and generous nature became an easy victim of unscrupulous people who imposed on his generosity. This, together with an unfortunate law suit in which he was involved, obliged him to dispose of the ancestral home. Some members of the family went to reside with the squire's eldest son William, who was then living at Ovingham Rectory. William, later Canon of Durham, was a distinguished antiquarian and author; another son, Francis, was the father of Colonel Greenwell; and another, Henry, being of a delicate nature, went abroad for health reasons. It is interesting to learn that Greenwell Ford was bought by the late Judge Greenwell in 1896 and is now the residence of Colonel Greenwell.

The two persons in whom we are most interested are Dorothy, better known as Dora, and her brother the Rev. Alan Greenwell, who was appointed first rector of Golborne when the church was built in 1849. In 1850, Miss Greenwell, her father, mother and brother came to Golborne and remained for four years. "This was a parish carved out of a neglected district" with a new church whose members were realising for the first time the benefits arising from a parish church. Previously, for over a century, the parishioners had had to go to Lowton chapel for worship. Now, religious societies were starting to develop in the township, and meeting places of various kinds became recognised. The manufacturing industry was in its infancy. Two cotton mills and a weaving shed existed and one, probably two, small mines at Edge Green, a hamlet on the verge of the township. Apart from agriculture these were the important industries. In these conditions an enormous amount of foundation work had to be done. Dora

Greenwell wholeheartedly assisted her brother in his numerous duties, but her father was in declining health, and the strain of nursing him began to tell on brother and sister. Then the father died. The rector resigned the living in 1854, and mother and sister returned to Durham where they lived together for eighteen years.

Now, after the lapse of a century, we are beginning to realise the importance and merit of so distinguished a writer as Dora Greenwell who in her earlier years lived in Golborne. It is regrettable that little direct evidence of her stay here survives; we are obliged to turn for information about her to her biographers.

Mr W. Dorling published his memoirs in 1885, and Miss Manyard, authoress of *The Life of Dora Greenwell* (1926), claims to have spent the greater part of twenty years contacting people and examining hundreds of letters before starting to write the life story of this versatile lady. It is to her that we are indebted for details about the years that Dora spent in Golborne. The late Dr. Henry Bett also published a small volume, and therein pays this compliment: "I have long been convinced that Dora Greenwell is one of our greatest devotional writers in the English language both as regards substance and style, yet her early books are mostly out of print, and seem to be known only to a small circle of admirers." The poet J.G. Whittier, when he first came in contact with her writings said "They are perhaps addressed too exclusively to those who minister in the inner sanctuary to be entirely intelligible to the vaster number who minister in the outer courts." Jean Ingelow, the poetess, pronounced her to be "the most remarkable woman she ever knew" and Dr. W. Robertson Nicoll declared her to be a great influence for good. He said he "owed her a debt that never could be repaid and that he had learned more theology from her than from any other teacher."

Miss Greenwell published her first volume of poems in 1848 and a second edition appeared in 1850; so one edition at least was published during her stay in Golborne.

"It was here that she rubbed off her shyness among the brusque independent people and acquired her pleasant manner with the poor; poor, not in material things alone, but in health, the friendless, forlorn, and unattractive beings hidden away here and there, which any one may find by looking for them." Although the years spent at Golborne may have been exacting they had their compensations, and she appears to have retained many happy memories of them as may be seen from the following letter written from the home of her old friend, Miss Moon.

Golborne Dale ,

*Ever since I came here I have improved in health and
have had such a beatific visit in all respects...
I was so low and suffering that it is a wonder I have
had so much enjoyment. This is a real cottage with
lattice windows and roses looking in at all of them
and my friend is very kind... Then we have Alan
as a neighbour for he has taken on a piece of duty in
a colliery district in the neighbourhood, what we
call mission work, forming an offset church in the
parish of an old friend with whom he is staying. I
cannot tell you what pleasure I have had among my
old friends gentle and simple, some very gentle and some
very simple. I did not think it possible they should
have remembered after so long separation and the
affection they have shown has been balm and wine
and marrow and fatness. It is a real affection, warm
personal regard of which as life wears on one gets
comparatively little, while of mere kindness there
is, happily, always plenty to be found. Some of the
girls are very pretty and some t'other way about
but people who can look and love so can do without
being pretty. The old people are quite as affectionate
in their own way, which is to sit a long time silent
looking at 'oo' as if 'oo' was some rare and beautiful
production of nature or art, and then to give a great
sigh between pleasure and regret, and then to say
some quaint thing as sweet as the vowels it is composed of.*

From this and other such writings we gather she was equally at home visiting the factory operatives in their homes or teaching in the Sunday school where, she narrates,

A History of Golborne

I have gone about delivering such homilies on morals and manners - the last being a rather low ebb - I have got my name up in the parish, and lord it over the boys in the school who are a rough set, that I fear I am acquiring a taste for domineering and hectoring...

Unfortunately, there are few portraits of Dora Greenwell in existence. The only known likeness is said to be at Greenwell Ford. At one period a few of her works appeared with an engraving as the frontispiece. In appearance, Dora Greenwell has been described as "tall, very slender, with a gentle hesitating manner and soft, cooing voice. A rather slim, dark woman of elegant, serious type with a particularly pleasing voice and mode of elocution. And such eyes; not black either, but dark, luminous brown eyes and wonderfully vivacious." Dora Greenwell belonged to that illustrious company of noble women of whom the world knows too little and to whom it owes so much. Remembering the age in which she lived when the new theories regarding evolution caused many people to flounder in a sea of uncertainty, she remained calm and unperturbed. Possibly this was in some measure due to a settled purpose of mind which found expression in the symbolism depicted on the front page of her many books, a design prepared by G.D. Leslie R.A. It was a flat Latin cross with the motto *Et teneo at teneor* - "I both hold and am held."

Although we feel the urge to quote extracts from her works and give a fuller description of her activities, the scope of this local history does not permit it. It is quite impossible here to describe her many attainments, for she was a woman of rich culture, extremely well read in French, German and English Literature. She quoted freely from the poets. Her books are mostly of a devotional character; *The Soul's Legend, The Two Friends, Carmen Crucis, Essays, The Covenant or Life and Peace*, together with a few volumes of poems. Some or these poems are still used as hymns today. She saw beauty in nature as well as in human character; the burnished leaves of autumn and the silence of the woods appealed to her.

It seems as if it never could be so lovely as it was yesterday. The wood so rich and scented, the meadows so warm and bronzed, the garden so still and enchanted in sunshine of the golden days gone before. The gossamer floats lightly in the air, the leaf reddens, the apple loosens its hold on the stalk, all is peace.

We are pleased to honour her memory and privileged to know that for a time she dwelt among us.

Chapter VII
Law and Order
Ecclesiastical Courts

When the church was the centre of village life its courts played an important part in the settlement of disputes. The ecclesiastical courts administered the canon law while the royal courts administered the common law. The Vestry Committee had the power to appoint, and approve the appointment of certain officials. It could also sanction decisions of the parish. Men went to church to transact business as well as to say prayers. The parson was often the agent of the lord of the manor and between them they constituted a miniature oligarchy.

Announcements relating to secular matters were occasionally made immediately after service. Business was discussed in the nave of the church and at times the manor courts were held there. Although the bishops disapproved of such practices, their protests were unavailing, so we need not be surprised to learn that:

> *At the pranouncement of the Amen in the evening*
> *service, the clerk would hasten to the steps of*
> *the sundial and announce in a loud voice to a*
> *departing congregation 'sales by auction' for*
> *the following week.*

During 1632-4 the chancellor and the archdeacon visited the district in connection with various church matters, and to hear presentments. Judged by present day practices, some of the matters dealt with appear trifling.

The complaints related to the laity, clergy, the sexton, sabbath breakers, absentees from church, married couples living apart, unmarried couples living together and persons working during service hours. In fact "whatever escaped through the sluices controlled by the justices was caught in the meshes of the archdeacon's net." Fines were imposed and the court could excommunicate the offender and deprive him of "the society of Christian men." The Archdeacon's Court was abolished in 1641 when the Long

Parliament launched its attack on the church on the eve of the Civil War. Although the court itself was revived at the Restoration, its former powers over the laity were not.

Presentments included non-observance of a saint's day, making bricks on the Sabbath and playing bowls while worship was being conducted. "Laymen of rank were presented because they sent for the blesser to bless cattle that were sick at Winwick." The blesser could not have been a veterinary surgeon because there were none. The incident suggests that something more than an ordinary ailment had to be contended with and may explain why the laymen resorted to what appears to be an almost superstitious practice. Yet was it any more superstitious than recognising plough Sunday and bringing the plough into church and praying for the blessing of its service?

A complaint was lodged against a woman "who knelt by a corpse set down by a Cross." We hesitate to make any observations on such a simple statement of fact, but it should be borne in mind that south west Lancashire was well known for its crosses. Where the cross in question stood is not mentioned: it could have been Fearnhead Cross, Hulme Cross or even Lowton Cross.

The Police

It has been estimated that during the seventeenth century there were ten thousand parishes in England, and it was the exception for a parish to have more than five hundred inhabitants. Some authorities state that three hundred was usual. Local government was usually in the hands of unpaid officials elected by the Court Leete. At this court, complaints or presentments as they were called, were made. They concerned trespass, breaking of fences, straying cattle, excessive prices for food, bakers who gave short weight, also people who dressed in material not in accordance with their station in life. Inspectors of meat, weights and measures, ale tasters, pound keepers, poachers, dog-whippers, constables and burleymen, and persons witholding suit and service came before the court. In 1859, Thomas Lawton, Baron of Newton, took action against certain Golborne tenents "for encroaching on waste land and witholding suit and service at the courts."

Every Hundred was bound to provide a high constable and every parish had to provide a petty constable. Because he had so many duties, the petty constable could delegate some of them to another person. The constable of Tudor times should not be compared with the constables of our day. The earlier constable of the vill or parish, according to reputable sources, has been repeatedly acknowledged by law "as belonging to one of the most ancient offices in the realm for conservation of peace." He had to see to the observance of law, and could prohibit the erection of a house or cottage in excess of the requirements of the district. He patrolled the streets carrying a lantern, a bunch of keys and a rattle, and pro-claimed the hour and the state of the weather.

It was not until after 1829 that the efficient force we now know came into being owing to the initiative of Robert Peel, from whose name the terms Bobbies and Peelers originated. These men carried truncheons and hand grips, and wore the familiar blue uniform and top hat. By 1856, it had been ordered that "every County and Borough employ a force" half local and half national. From that time, we have had an efficient, paid police force. When it was the duty of every parish to provide for its own poor, the constable co-operated with the church wardens in administering the Poor Law. Woe betide any unfortunate migrant who strayed into the parish seeking relief, for all such persons were liable to be whipped severely and passed from constable to constable until the place of their birth was reached.

"The poor ye have with you always" so it was said, but: "We don't keep them here long!" On the instructions received from the Justices, the constable saw to the whipping of offenders. If children were ordered to be whipped, the parent might carry out the sentence in the presence of the officer. If the parent declined, then the officer obliged.

Certain reports had to be prepared for the Justices. Many of these had such in common with present-day official forms and stated such facts as:

> *The poore are provided for, the Stocks and Whipping*
> *Post are in good repair, warrants executed, hues*
> *and cries have been pursued, highways and bridges*
> *in repair, and all things belonging to my office*
> *are in good order to the best of my knowledge.*

Roger Lowe shows that Golborne had such a constable. The entry for August 20,1664 states:

Constables of Haddock and Golebourne came to me
to have me write their presentments for assizes,
and when I had donne I writt:-

"The poore is provided, highways repaired,
their queries answered and the clerk
unrewarded,"

at which they laughed most heartily.

We are unable to say precisely when the first police officer was appointed to Golborne - possibly towards the end of 1850. Even so, there were no suitable premises wherein to confine a wrong-doer. Later, in March 1864, a meeting of the Parish and Parochial Committee agreed upon the following proposal:

That a memorial should be drawn and presented to the
Chief Constable, Captain Elgee of Preston requesting
that a lockup in Golborne should be provided for the
use of the County Constabulary and for public welfare."

Evidently the memorial was complied with and the first lock-ups were provided in the Police Station in Queen Street.

The Village Stocks

In 1374, the Commons "prayed" for stocks to be established in every village and later every parish had its own stocks. These were usually set up in a public place on the village green or near the parish church. Some were of a movable type; others were permanent. Their purpose was to humiliate those who offended against the law by confining them for a number of hours. The local stocks near the entrance gate to St. Luke's Church, Lowton, are not the original pair. Whether they, like the chapel, served both townships is uncertain. Our Diarist of almost three centuries ago makes this entry:

A History of Golborne

There was a horse race runne from Golborne Stocks to Ashton. I got a horse and ran with them.

The question arises: Where did the stocks stand? To this we have no answer. We had no village green and no village church in those days. The most likely place would have been Golborne Smithies, for there several roads converged. In the absence of definite information, we may surmise that the farmstead known as *Stack House* which adjoined these roads was the most likely public place, and that Stack has been substituted for Stock.

Village Stocks typical of those which stood in Golborne

Chapter VIII
Sports and Pastimes

Even when hours of labour were long, some time was found for sport. Lack of transport and low wages prevented people from travelling far afield, and so they were accustomed to find their recreation near to where they worked and lived. Their pastimes did not change much through the ages; bowling, foumart-hunting, horse-racing and cock-fighting remained the most popular. "Hawkeries in the woods" wrote the Domesday recorder: we may include falconry, deer hunting and, at a later period, fox hunting and hare coursing as local sports.

It is said of King John that he had in Lancashire alone upwards of three hundred game cocks reserved for sport. It is not surprising therefore to learn that cock-fighting was freely indulged in on Saturday afternoons at Winwick with the sanction of the clergy. The old cock-pit at Newton under the shadow of the church was well patronised. The local historian relates that the old Lord Derby and old Colonel Legh matched their birds to fight a main on a Sunday after-noon. Possibly the Golborne patrons may have argued that under such distinguished patronage they too could indulge in the same sport, and Ward's Barn became the scene of similar events.

Various smallholders in and around the township bred game birds and continued the practice of making them tough by the revolting process of cutting off their wattles and feeding them back to the bird, which was promptly killed if it squawked.

In other parts of the county, his lordship's cock cart might have been seen festooned with white bags each containing a bird. These were being distributed among the tenantry to be kept until required. The sport continued regardless of prohibitions and the village constable was helpless to restrain the practice.

It is surmised that the Rev. Charles Herle was interested in race-horses, for in a letter written about 1650 to Richard Legh of Lyme to whom he was tutor, he states:

*Yr coltes are I heare very well at Bradley, soe are
not myne but all extreamly troubled with strangle yet
the Kirk stands in the Kirkyard still and I remayne
exceeding ill at this time. Sir yr most humble and
obliged servant C. Herle.*

Information relating to horse racing is rather fragmentary. The Newton Common race track existed about 1680. There the race for the Old Newton Cup originated before being transferred to that popular rendezvous of racing enthusiasts - Haydock Park. Haydock Park is on the verge of the township and was mainly farmland until 1880 when it was taken over for hare coursing. The promoters do not appear to have had a very successful return for their outlay and later The Haydock Park Race Company took over about one hundred acres to make what is at the present time one of the finest courses in the North of England.

Inns

Many leisure hours have been spent in the local inns. The inn is a natural concomitant of the road. It provided an essential service for man and beset as trade and transport developed. The earliest inns were built round a court-yard. A balcony ran round the walls several feet above ground level and this was divided into sections for the convenience of traders and travellers. Under it, divisions were made for animals. Travellers might at times find the upper rooms occupied, and so they had to contrive a resting place along with, or near to, the animals.

Macaulay writing of the Stuart period says "houses were not numbered or named, there would be no use in doing so, for only a small proportion of London's errand boys, porters and coachmen could read. It was necessary to use marks which the most ignorant could understand. Shops and inns were distinguished by painted and sculptured signs which gave a gay and grotesque aspect to the streets. The walk between Charing Cross and Whitechapel lay between an endless succession of Saracen's Heads, Royal Oaks, Blue Lions and Golden Lambs which disappeared when no longer required."

A selection of signs from the numerous inns in use can throw additional light on some parts of a township's history. The Jolly Thresher relates to the days when heresy hunts were in progress and the head of the house of de Trafford, to hide from his pursuers, dressed himself as a labourer and armed with a threshel, flailed away at the sheaves of corn to the cry of *Now Thus.* The enquirers evidently concluded that the fellow was a half wit, and went away. We have the legend of the house of Stanley which has given rise to the sign of the Eagle and Child called by the locals The Brid and Babby.

Golborne appears to have had an excessively large number of inns, for at one period these and other licenced houses were out of all proportion to the needs of the inhabitants. Some inns were practically side by side; others were grouped in a bunch or were separated only by the width of a street. The Queen Anne and The Cross Keys were next to each other. The Royal Oak was only a short distance from the Sir Charles Napier which was next to the Prince or Wales, with the New Inn across the street. A story I collected about the naming of the Sir Charles Napier is worthy of recording. My informant stated: "After the house was built, an ex-serviceman, Lance Corporal Tom Edwards was selected by the owners as a prospective tenant and they suggested to him that he might name the house. On reflection he replied 'I'll name it after my late commanding officer, Sir Charles Napier'." The choice was a commendable one if only for this reason, Sir Charles Napier was the first English general who ever recorded in his dispatches the names of private soldiers who had distinguished themselves side by side with their officers. The Railway Hotel supplanted the tavern known as the Railway Tavern. The Manor Arms was near The Signs in the Cellar, with the Church Inn on the opposite side of the street. One old resident remembering past days rather facetiously explained to me that The Signs in the Cellar were the barrels of beer which had the peculiar property of running when approached. Possibly he meant 'broached' but only being a novitiate I preferred not to argue the 'pint' with him.

Amongst the names we have an assortment of Arms; The Brickmakers, The Spinners, The Manor, The Assessors and The Legh. The Brickmakers was appropriate when brickmaking flourished. The Spinners can readily be associated with a factory. Certain names, The Victoria and The Royal show another influence in the choosing of names. The Queen Anne appears to be a long established house. Formerly it was the Queen's Head, at least when Andrew Sconce was the licensee in 1774. For what reason the name was changed we have not been able to ascertain. Possibly a queen deprived of her body was a displeasing thought to those who later occupied the house, and so the name was altered to that of Queen Anne.

Our Lion is a red one which has no connection with the one of the prophetic order which lay down with the lamb. The nearest affinity was The Ram which has suffered extinction all but The Horns. Nearly two hundred years ago there was a mill, probably a corn mill, near the brook in Harvey Lane. At one time John Peters was the occupier, He held "thirty-seven acres of land, a mill-garden and a mill kiln as well as a dam of water." It is not unlikely that the inn known as the Millstone derived its name from this mill. Some inns of similar name have appropriately had a millstone built into the wall.

The name Angel given to one of the inns in existence by the early nineteenth century is most intriguing. Why it was so named no one appears to know definitely. It may have been the result of developments in Edge Green. In the 1820's Edge Green was a hamlet with probably not more than thirty cottages all told in the vicinity of the first coal mines of the township. As in surrounding townships, there was a riotous, unruly and dangerous element abroad. Such names as Hell Nook, Dam Lane and Glory Row are suggestive. John Wesley and other notable people who travelled in the district recorded their impressions. Wesley refers to the "unruly crowd at Wigan," and Downall Green was said to be "a town wicked to a proverb; we had a specimen of its inhabitants in the behaviour of the man who met us and who accosted us with such language as would have become the inhabitants of the bottomless pit."

Several years later William Alexander records his visit to Edge Green where he found the people "wicked and beastly intemperate" and the place "the scene of many fights." But Alexander was not dismayed and later his visits were fruitful. The unruly element became subdued, sober and "peaceful as a little child," so much so, that people who did not believe such a change was possible were known to have crept to the windows of cottages in the darkness just to see how the inmates, particularly the desperate characters, were behaving. Again quoting Mr Alexander: "The people here are about to build a school and chapel. A miner has subscribed £10 and a publican £5. Even though the hope of his gains was diminished it speaks well for the publican who was prepared to range himself "on the side of the Angel."

Customs

Customs hang upon us with a weight
heavy as frost and deep almost as life.

Customs originated amongst the first communities. Now in the twentieth century, we find it difficult to evade them as they still affect our daily life in various ways.

Relating to questions upon which the law is silent, resort is usually made to custom. Certain privileges have come to be recognised and called "the custom of the country," inaccurately so, for it would have been nearer the truth to have called them "the custom of the district," since they differ from place to place.

Reliance on custom alone is beset with difficulties. It must be uninterrupted as a right even though it may have fallen into disuse; and it must not conflict with other customs, nor be uncertain in operation.

It is to Hugh-de-Bracton that we are indebted for disentangling from the strange mixture of Saxon and Norman customs what is now referred to as a legal system. When feudalism prevailed, the occupation of land and the defence of the nation was buttressed by custom. An example of this is Thomas de Golborne paying one third of a knight's fee in substitution of personal service to the crown. The lords of the land held it on conditions of service, and persons who held land from thee were bound to render service by bearing arms. "We may detect at an early period a change in custom, for by statute of Edward I free men were enabled to sell any part of their land - a privilege not previously allowed - but the purchaser of the lands was compelled to hold them under the chief lord of the fee by the same service and customs as they had been held by the vendor." Land laws are full of complexity and can best be left to lawyers to be dealt with. The ancient tenures reveal some astonishing terms. For example: "This messuage (small holding) is held by X in free and common socage by a yearly rent or one pair of gloves and 2/-" or "one third of a peppercorn rent," or "one red rose." Coming nearer to our own times leases are to be found containing clauses by which the tenant agrees to give one day's service carting turf or ploughing, or to keep a couple of hounds, a spaniel or a game cock, in addition to paying the rent. In other leases certain customs are to be observed although nothing is mentioned in the agreement. Such a condition could be construed as applying to service in the Lancashire Hussars. Several of the large estate owners expected their tenants to provide a man or a horse, or both, according to the acreage occupied by a tenant. In this way, a company of troopers, Yeomanry or Hussars was formed. All the men and horses from the townships of Newton, Haydock, Golborne, Ashton, St. Helens, Lathom, Scarisbrick and other places assembled annually for ten days training at Southport in the month of May. Several of them served in the South African War, and at the coronation of King Edward VII both men and horses formed a guard of honour along the coronation route.

An old custom was connected with the practice of marling. Marl is a kind of clay containing lime and long before liming of land became a practice, marl supplied the lime. Not only did it increase the crops, it also gave body to light land. In the year 1225, an act was passed stating that "Every man has a right to sink a marly pit on his own ground." For several centuries the marling of land was a common practice. Indeed many farmers had no option, as some tenancy agreements show that the tenant was obliged to marl. So we are accustomed to seeing these pits on almost every farm in the township.

The practice was noticed by our diarist. He writes:

> *May. Munday 1664. I went to Roger Wainwright to*
> *Nicholas Burscoes marle pitt and*
> *gave marlers a quarter of tobacco.*

A rather curious custom obtained among the marlers. The chief digger was called "the lord of the soil" and when a favourable occasion arose, he would stand on the brink of the pit and cry "0 Yez, O Yez, O Yez! this is to give notice that Mr... has given us marlers part of one thousand pounds and to whomsoever will do the same, we will give thanks and shout." The men engaged in the task would then join hands and cry together "Largesse, Largesse, Largesee!"

Golborne had a lime kiln in existence almost two hundred years ago. The

Bank Heath Award refers to it thus: "One small portion of land lying in the lane near Golborne town in which a lime kiln is lately erected, forty-eight yards by seven in breadth, subject to a rent of sixpence a year." Similar kilns operated in Astley and Bedford for the burning of the Sutton or Terras lime from beds of magnesium limestone or the permian strata.

Another local custom was the recognition of May Day. This was indeed more than local, it was national; even royalty collected May dew as beauty charm.

With the alteration of the calendar in 1752, May Day was eleven days earlier that the original "First O' May." Up to the first decade of the twentieth century the practice of turning out cattle from their winter quarters on the twelfth day of May was almost religiously adhered to. Instances are on record where livestock were turned out to grass one day earlier than the prescribed day. This was treated as an offence, and the owner was fined.

May Day revels commenced with the Morris dancers who assembled at Lowton church and paraded throughout the district. In other places May Poles were erected around which the villagers danced throughout the day. There were cart-horse parades, with the horses beribboned and decorated with gleaming chains and brasses, tinkling bells and polished harness - a custom still recognised in various towns. The children sang: "Here we come gathering nuts in May," "nuts" possibly being a misapplication for "knots" of May." A special festival in honour of the May Queen developed from these celebrations.

The first May Queen Festival in Golborne was held in 1880, the principal promoter being Mr Alfred Caunce, a local tradesman. The children taking part marched in procession along Park Vue, Legh Street and High Street and returned to a field kindly lent by Mr John Caunce where a May-pole had been erected around which the youngsters danced and sang the National Anthem. Miss Jane Waddington was the Queen of the May and the ceremony passed off without a single mishap. Afterwards the youngsters were regaled with buns and tea; everyone was seemingly very happy and great praise was given to the promoters. Visitors attended from miles around and the event, being something of an innovation as well as a success, the idea of making it an annual event developed. As it continued to attract an ever increasing number of visitors, various side shows were added; swings, round-abouts, aunt Sallys, plaiting the May-pole, climbing the greasy pole and other novelties.

One attraction of special interest was Billy Jackson's Clogwollopers. Eight boys, all of them under fourteen years of age, dressed in white shirts, black pants and gilded clogs, with straw hats perched on the back of their heads, gave a display of clog-dancing. Besides this, they played the part of clowns and performed tricks on a penny-farthing bicycle. After giving displays at local events, the party was invited to Blackpool for the season where they performed on the Central Pier and at the Tower. From Blackpool they went to London and performed at various Music Halls. Whilst in London, part of the time was spent at St. Mary's School, South Kensington, where they made the acquaintance of the inimitable Charlie Chaplin. He too wished to become a clog dancer and was trained as a reserve for the party. Even in those early days Charlie was a recognised mimic and used to imitate every artist on the bill. After touring the country for a time, the party broke up. A few of them, however, kept together and later visited Australia, France, Germany and Russia.

Simnel Sunday or Mothering Sunday continues to be observed. The observance of the Candle Cup has almost died out. The Merry Meal, as it is sometimes called, is in effect a mild form of carousal held to celebrate the birth of a child.

Customs relating to funerals are many. At one time crosses were erected to indicate resting places. Where no cross had been set up one was painted on the side of a house. These were necessary, as funerals sometimes meant a journey of thirty miles with twenty or more bearers. The funeral procession of the Earl of Derby in 1572 was three miles long. At the funeral of Sir Peter Legh, 1635, the cortege left Lyme for Winwick, a journey of thirty miles, with priests carrying torches and chanting dirges, and several hundred mourners in attendance. Bidding cards are now seldom seen. At best they are gruesome objects. It was the custom to invite persons to an internment by presenting one of these cards to the bidden. Two persons would go together to the home of the bidden, each wearing a sprig of rosemary and would present the card. At the house of the deceased inheritance ale, also known as arval ale, would be dispensed, and the one succeeding to the estate would sit near the door to receive some small contribution from the invited persons. After the last rites and ceremonies, the funeral party would adjourn to a nearby inn to receive light refreshment, spiced ale or wine and biscuits and cheese. The return journey might well be one of several miles, and refreshment was a necessity. Roger Lowe writes on 16 December, 1666: "I went to the funeral of Ann Taylor who was married to Ralph Ashton in Abram, and I went fasting from home, so at noon when we had buried the corpse and expected according to custom to have some refreshment, nothing being servied with much vexation I got to Ashton with a hungry belly."

For long journeys the horse litter was sometimes used, and later the shillibier. Golborne had a public shillibier, usually kept at a tradesman's shop and residence at Bank Heath. It was a fearsome object. No wonder the children dreaded the sight of it when it was surmounted with the feathery plumes known as dollies. There were black horses with long flowing manes and tails, and the mourners in black, with black-bordered handkerchiefs. Yards of crepe were attached to the men's hats and reached down their backs. And those silk hats previously sponged with cold tea and meticulously smoothed with a silk cloth. It appeared as if one person vied with another in producing the most depressing effect. Such was the custom.

There was a time, on the decease of a person, when it was usual to visit the home of the bereaved. Usually a company would go together to offer sympathy. On all such occasions the ritual was to offer visitors wine, lemonade, or spiced ale and biscuits or cake. Whether the visitor came from a sense of sympathy or morbidity it is difficult to say. One person whose wife had passed on evidently became so annoyed by the visitors that he vowed he would effect a cure and at the same time gain a little peace and privacy. He decided upon a rather unusual expedient. It was to bore a hole through the floorboards of the room where the deceased lay. From the room below he passed a rod long enough to reach the pillows of the bed.

Toward evening the ritual commenced. Some half dozen people assembled in the bedroom and recited the usual comments and adulations. "Aye, an her wur a good sooart; an don't ur look like-like..." Whereupon, the deceased sat up and nodded assent. The effect can be better imagined than described. Safety was in flight, and one and all left the room with inordinate haste. After that there were no more visits.

Certain customs are associated with the different seasons. The time of year, when children play their various games is settled by custom. Children, in the days before motor cars were so sommon, used to occupy both the pavements and the roadway playing whip and top, or peg top, hopscotch, battledore, skipping rope, marbles and other games; they all emerged as the days of spring drew near. Most of the games survive. Valentine's Day has a deal of romance attached to it, and one resident has a collection of Valentines which go back for about a century. The chocolate eggs, so prominent at Easter-tide, are reminiscent of the pace-eggers. Easter also brings hot cross buns with the superstition that bread and cakes baked on Good Friday can be kept as a cure for various ailments, or, if kept for the year, serve as a protection against fire. At Christmas, the parties of carol singers still set out. When harvests were reaped with the sickle, it was said that the corn spirit lodged in the last few remaining straws to be cut. The reaper would throw the sickle and sever the straws and the harvester would rush forward crying "A neck, a neck." The straws were gathered, plaited into a design known as the corn dolly. This was kept in a prominent place in the house as a guarantee of good luck for the next harvest. Some of these old practices are based in part upon superstitious ideas.

Superstitions

According to ancient mythology the earliest people appear to have believed that numerous deities presided over the affairs of mankind. The Greeks believed that the god Pan ruled over the universe. The winged Nemesis rode upon a stag. Ceres presided over the fruits of the earth. Her daughter, Prosperine, was captured and carried away by Pluto to the dark regions to be liberated during the Spring whilst returning for the Winter. The days of the week were appointed to separate deities. Man became imbued with the belief that the gods could be offended by sins of omission or commission, and could be appeased by gifts.

These crude ideas once having established themselves were fostered and nourished in numerous ways, and even in this enlightened age a surprisingly large number of people have a secret regard for these pagan beliefs. While we may smile at the foibles and follies of our ancestors we continue to cherish the old delusions with a fanatic faith and cling to them to the last. We pay homage to Lady Luck. If something happens to our advantage it is our lucky day. If we bank on something which we believe will be to our advantage and lose it then it is because our luck is out. But to make quite sure that bad luck will not intervene we keep our fingers crossed or touch wood. To prevent malign influence having effect we are told that a special piece of wood should be worn next to the skin, or a piece of camphor, the sacramental shilling, a potato, a four leaf clover, or the effigy of a black cat. Motorists carry a winged Mercury on the car bonnet or a pictured saint in the rear window. The waggoner of the past affixed diamond and crescent shaped amulets to the harness of his horses to ward off the evil eye.

In numerous instances we notice horse-shoes attached to doors and buildings even though it all seems so ridiculous; superstition is still ingrained in the majority of people. The first Good Friday cannot be forgotten. A house-wife would not start spring-cleaning on a Friday. Numerous country folk would not entertain the idea of beginning a new task on a Friday. Most unlucky is the Friday which happens to fall on the thirteenth day of the month. ·

Thirteen at table is a bad omen so to obviate the ill luck a trencher guest is invited. Some hotels and hospitals omit room thirteen.

"Don't look back when you commence a journey, it's unlucky"; we are told to "remember Lot's wife." So the way to neutralize the evil spell is to cast salt over the left shoulder. It must be the left one for there the Evil One lurks. Beware of walking under a ladder or breaking a mirror. The howling dog and hooting owl are ominous. If a pynot (magpie) crosses your path correct its foreboding by making the sign of the cross on the ground.

Even the witches always found some excuse for not entering a house or not casting a spell on the householder where a piece of wood lay as a cross over the threshold. Why were gargoyles on churches and old rags on draw wells but to break the spell of witches?

Numerous admonitions relate to the New Year and Christmastide. A dark haired person must be the first to enter the house in the New Year if good luck is to prevail.

Every age has its superstitions some of which have survived for a long time. Though strong-minded people believe in cause and effect the shallow-minded believe in luck, or the accident of birth, being swayed by a particular planet or the stars in their courses. However dogmatic a person may be about a superstitious belief this is not a valid reason for accepting his conclusions. The venerable John Wesley, great though he was, went so far as to say "giving up belief in witchcraft is in effect giving up the Bible." Even today there are those who believe in witchcraft.

May Day Celebrations

Psychology explains much that was once regarded as mysterious. As an example of the power of suggestion and superstition we may take an example from the will of Hamlet Mather of Manchester (Manchester Wills 1573-1639): "I give and bequeath to...the goulde I received of the King's Majestie." The gold referred to was a half sovereign given to him by Charles I. It was declared to be a specific remedy against scrofula, a glandular disease known as King's Evil. In the days of the Stuarts the gift was freely made and certain days were appointed for the healing of the sick. A special service was included in the Prayer Book where it remained until the accession of George I. The sick were introduced by a surgeon to His Majesty who stroked the ulcers and swellings and hung a gold coin around the patient's neck. After this touching the chaplain said "They shall lay their hands on the sick and they shall recover." It is said that King James I touched eight hundred persons in the choir of Chester Cathedral. So we have royalty, surgeons and clergy alike condoning a superstitious practice.

Rush Bearing, an Old Lancashire Tradition

Chapter IX
Local Sayings and Writings
Dialect

A writer describing Lancashire dialect in 1662 maintained: "it is remarkably broad," and the Lancashire Saxon ancestry in the south and south-east of the county is still spoken in great perfection.

It is questionable whether, nowadays many native dwellers can fully comprehend the dialect for the keen edged phrases, a one-time speciality, are rapidly disappearing and giving place to standard English. But dialect is part of our common heritage and is far more meaningful and appropriate than most of the slang terms and modern colloquialisms we are accustomed to hear.

Persons unaccustomed to hearing it spoken are often bewildered by the peculiar words and phrases and even those of us who have been conversant with it from infancy hear words familiar, to our ancestors, but puzzling to ourselves. An old lady of my boyhood days used to say: "Good things are too good to keep to yer sen, they're like a bag o'nougars, beawnt ta boke eawt some weer." Only in later years did I learn that nougars, presumably a corruption of augers, was a term used for gimlets.

In the later part of the nineteenth century one frequently heard master and man conversing in dialect with an amazing familiarity. It was candid and direct speech, without anything servile or patronising about it; a familiarity respected by both parties. A most commendable trait of character was the consistency and trust reposed in a promise. When a man gave his word it was also his bond. It was reliable contract and could be summed up in a still prevalent word *jannock,* a word supposed to have been introduced by Flemish weavers, many of whom settled in south Lancashire. It related to jannock bread. This was made mainly of whole meal flour and the term signified no adulterants used, no chemicals introduced to bleach it and give it an unnatural appearance. Hence *jannock* signifies dependable, reliable, genuine, a 'gradely' commodity. Applied to a person's character it is a high compliment.

Brief mention may be made of a few recognised authorities on dialect. The Rev. W. Gaskell, M.A., made it a special study. Tim Bobbin, a schoolmaster, son of an Eccles clergyman; Edwin Waugh, a minute observer with extensive knowledge of the subject; Bamford and Brierly, together with others, revelled in the subject. Dora Greenwell mentions an interesting feature of Golborne history of over one hundred years ago in a letter: "I wish I could tell you what delightful little galas we have had here for the young men and maidens of the village. Concerts and recitations, and some of them can act with inimitable humour and spirit, - comic scenes which they study and get up among themselves; it seems a talent peculiar to Lancashire." At the time, and for long afterwards, comic scenes and dialect sketches were a usual feature of all such parties.

Some of the expressions reveal aspects of life, for example the privation and suffering experienced by young and old.

Edwin Waugh writes: "When I asked a villager whether Gommershaw boggart was ever seen now, he said 'Naw, we 'h niver see'n no boggerts neaw, nobbut when th' bradfleghs empty'." The bradflegh was a wooden frame criss-crossed with string on which the oat cakes were placed. It usually hung from the ceiling.

Ben Brierly also depicts the suffering among the children: "I've known th' lad set at th' loom weh a stick et side on 'im fort keep childer fro atin his sowse, them wur so clemmed." "Th' lad" was the parent; and sowse was a mixture of flour and water which, as a hand-loom weaver, he used for sizing the warps.

Even though confronted with insuperable difficulties the people showed a pathetic affection such as that which is so admirably portrayed in *Thar't welcome Bonnie Brid* and *Come whom ta thi childer and meh*. Someone may say: "Such things didn't happen here." Yet things did happen here which are equally sad: there's not much joy in potato soup, batter cakes, brewis, buttermilk porridge, curds and whey or sparrow pie. When I asked a man "How often did you have tea when you were a boy?" he said "Only ar folk ed tay, and they only had it onct a wek. Us childer ust ta sit on sackin' et frunt at fire weh a mug o' 'ot watter un a spoon full o' black trackle in it: that wur ar tay."

The word temse, so often misunderstood, is a south Lancashire word and applies to a small sieve which was used for screening ground corn or for similar service. When the quern was used the temse was a necessity. A person using it by a quick rotary movement could gather the husks together and remove them. To do the job to perfection required energy and skill but the slow lackadaisical person was considered "too slow to set the temse on fire." Thames evidently has been substituted for temse and it is a misnomer. This local word reminds us of local proverbs.

Local Proverbs

From the earliest times proverbs have been common. Although they are no longer usual ornaments of conversation they have not ceased to be treasuries of thought. In the past, however, besides being a condensed form of wisdom they took the place of books when scrolls and manuscripts were possessed by the few and books were almost unknown.

Golborne has few proverbs of purely local origin perhaps because of its being a small community: in 1801 when the first census was taken there were probably only 130 families here with limited contacts. Conversations with some of the oldest inhabitants have produced a number of sayings and proverbs principally in dialect. Some of them are traceable to other parts of the county. It may be of interest to record some, however, before they are lost.

The weather-wise - and so many operations depended in the past on the weather - who were particularly observant of the formation of the clouds, the flight of birds, the habits of cattle in the fields, the region of the wind, and the phases of the moon, accumulated numerous sayings. Some of the observations were dependable, but that cannot be said of all. Billinge Hill for example, given a fair day, can be seen from various positions in the township. If the weather is likely to be fair the hill is clearly defined, but;

> *If Billinge Hill puts on her hood*
> *Be sure the weather will not be good.*

Rivington Pike, some fourteen miles away, may stand out clear with roads and buildings discernible, but in this instance the clear view is not regarded with favour -

A History of Golborne

*If Rivington pike should stand out clear
Rain is not Far off we fear,*

Elsewhere in the county the opposite view is taken;

*If Rivington do wear a hood
Be sure the day will ne're be good.*

A proverb I recall having heard once was spoken by a veteran some fifty years ago. Then, implements and tools wars not so common as at present and borrowing was frequent. To journey six or seven miles for this purpose was not unusual, but the old man was desirous to impress upon me that borrowing often led to carelessness and that having a new tool I should take special care of it. He said " A tool of your own has a horn haft," meaning that "Borrowing dulls the edge of husbandry."

The colloquial flavour of other proverbs makes them distinctive. They cover all phases of human experience, marriage for instance: "It's better to marry o'er the mixen than o'er the moor." This may account for the frequency of consanguineous marriages, one aim of which was keeping money in the family. Many a village feud testifies to the prevalence of intermarriage, for it was said: "If tha hits one, tha hits th' lot." As the youth excused himself by saying: She's a pretty wench," the mother testily replied "her's monny a pratty nowt." Though beauty may be held to be "only skin deep" this saying is countered by "ugliness goes to th' booan."

Sometimes the performance of a good deed has unexpected results. Although "one good turn deserves another" this does not invariably follow. It is annoying to find "you've given your loaf to beg your shive" (crust) to which could also be added "etten bread is soon forgeeten." The parents who were agreeably surprised to receive a gift from their son were wont to say "it's not often the kitlin brings a mouse to th'owd cat."

Sudden prosperity has often had ill effects for "it takes a steady hand to carry a full cup" and "some folks, like horses cannot stand keep" being inclined "to kick o'er the traces." Hence also the saying: "Clogs, and clogs; then boots, and then clogs again." Ill-gotten gains are sarcastically referred to by "what comes o'er the divil's back goes back under his belly." Other local proverbs are:

Think twice before you choose, you can only pick once,
so you may as well have an apple as a crab.

Fine faces fill no cubborts, nor feaw 'uns no butteries.

And and a fair way to divide a cake is:

You cut and I'll choose or I'll cut and you choose.

At least a score of sayings concern restitution: "For the wrongs we have committed a kind of avenging deity is content to wait until age has chilled our bones and made us unfit to fight or flee and then turns up with the unpaid account." Some call it Fate, others Nemesis. This proverb is universal: *"Whatsoever a man sows he reaps."* It is said that: *"Wild oats me that bitter bread is to be eaten."* The local saying has it: *"If he doesn't get you comin' he'll get you when you'r coming back."*

Nicknames

We have an abundance of nicknames and it has become a common practice to refer to persons by such names instead of by the correct ones. Nicknames like a burr have an unpleasant way of sticking closely when applied. Generally they relate to a personal peculiarity, occupation, or even residence. When brickmaking was common in the township Jen o'th Hill and Scotch Bob were well known by those names. What their correct names were we do not know. Dodger, Cudge, Black-Jack or Johnny-One-Speed were also people best known by nicknames. Owd Felly was the local carrier. He built up a business carting coals to hamlets on the way to Warrington and on the return journey would have a collection of parcels to deliver. For this service he charged 'tuppence' - this at a time when a glass of beer cost three halfpence.

A local publican intent on showing his smartness decided to take a rise out of Felly. "Tuppence did you say?" he asked on receipt of the parcel, "'Will a glass o' beer do instead?" Felly hesitated. He looked at the questioner as if he might have been an art treasure and said: "Aye, a glass o' beer un a a'penny." Whatever else he was or was not, Felly believed it was possible to make pennies out of a'pennies, and if anyone chided him he would retort: "If folk 'av as much pleasure eh spendin a bit o' brass us I

113

have eh gettin it, eh don't begrudge um."

Nicknames have been applied to places as well as persons. A stranger might ask for a person's house and would be confused by the answer that so-and-so lived in the Salt-box Row, or Monkey Roost or Ten Row. Glory Row, the Smoothing-iron and Donkey Row were equally puzzling names.

A Local Diarist: Roger Lowe

In writing this local history the diary of Roger Lowe has proved invaluable. Lowe wrote in the seventeenth century at the same time that Pepys was writing his more famous diary. Lowe's diary does not appear to have been brought to public notice till 1876 when J. P. Earwaker quoted excerpts from it in *Local Gleanings*. The following year, J. Rose, F.H,S. published the diary complete in the *Leigh Chronicle*. The original manuscript is now in the Hindley Municipal Library.

Roger Lowe of Ashton-in-Makerrield was apprenticed to Thomas Hammond, a Leigh mercer, who had a shop in Ashton and appointed Lowe to take charge of it. Why Lowe kept a diary is not known, possibly because he noticed many interesting things and interesting people in the district and was desirous of retaining the experience.

In the seventeenth century writing was an accomplishment shared only by the few, as may be perceived from some of the entries. Lowe was called upon to complete articles of apprenticeship, make wills and prepare the constables reports for the assizes; even the most intimate matters relating to courtship were committed to him.

In the course of business Lowe travelled between Ashton, Warrington, Chester, Leigh, Wigan, and sometimes he visited Manchester and Liverpool. Occasionally he journeyed on horseback but chiefly on foot, leaving the shop apparently in charge of John Craddock, a co-apprentice.

Lowe was of an affable disposition and on good terms with most people. Being known as a reliable person and as one who could keep his own counsel he was entrusted by many people with their private affairs. He was not averse to combining business with pleasure and mentions "going to hear organes at Winwicke and Chester." He visited the burial ground at

Wigan and, finding a skull above ground, made it his business to find someone to bury it. He loved a game of bowls, hunted the pole-cat and would go to see a cock-fight, or a horse race.

Although he does not refer to matters of national importance and fails to mention directly, for instance, the Act of Uniformity, he makes a note of going to hear an ejected minister preach, and of journeying to a chapel (ry) to hear a bishop. When in the mood after a service he would betake himself to an adjoining inn where he repeated the discourse for the benefit of his cronies. Why he should go to Ashton Heath and kneel in a ditch to say prayers, or go to the Town Green to read and sing, is difficult to comprehend. He mentions being sent for by a dying woman to offer prayers for her.

It is from his varied and interesting entries made between 1663 and 1676 that we are able to reconstruct something of the way the people lived here two and a hair centuries ago, and an otherwise unimportant man is remembered.

Chapter X
Analecta

Anyone who is prepared to deal with historical gleanings and will take the trouble to separate the wheat from the chaff will be amply repaid by the discovery of interesting events. Possibly someone will be sufficiently interested in the life of our ancestors to continue research into matters which have only been hinted at here. Mention must be made of the generous gift by Lord Newton of a playing field, familiarly known from the time when Golborne had a successful team as the Cricket Field. It is on this field that the War Memorial was erected in memory of those who made the supreme sacrifice in the First World War.

Nor can we overlook the changes in local government. The Urban District of Golborne was formed on 31st December 1894. With the abolition of the Leigh Rural District Council, Lowton, part of Glazebury Kenyon, Culcheth and Holcroft were included in the township of Golborne in 1933. Such an expansion in municipal affairs made the diminutive offices in Worsley Street unsuitable. The U.D.C. accepted the kindly offer of the premises known as Lyme House Lowton. These are set in surroundings in keeping with the combined interests of the joint townships. A most generous gift was made by Councillor Robert Allen J.P. who presented a Chairman's Chain of Office to the Council in the same year.

In the affairs of the township we have tried to keep as near as possible to all those who have interested themselves in the land and the people. We felt the necessity of indicating a wider field where history, tradition and romance could be investigated. For want of a better illustration we may speak figuratively of the spokes of a wheel, with Golborme as the hub. Proceeding from the hub in any direction we may find history, legend or romance. In Cromwell's time there was the eventful battle of Wigan Lane and the rout of the Duke of Hamilton's forces; the pursuit and regrouping at Cop Hill and Red Bank the siege of Winwick Hall and the church. Some soldiers charged with insubordination were treated as rebels and hanged in the Gallows Croft. There are several stories of the Bradshaws of Haigh, of the quarrels and flight of Bradshaw to the Continent and his unexpected reappearance. This was followed by his pursuit of his rival who had made overtures to the Lady Mabel. As a result of this a duel took place opposite Newton Park. This spot is marked by a stone in the footpath - the Bloody Stone - on which the bloodstains are said to be permanent.

By another line we may approach Birchley Hall, Billinge. It was there that Roger Anderton of Lostock and Billinge set up a private printing press. He is regarded as "the father of Lancashire printing." W.E. Axon states: "There were in Lancashire in Elizabeth's days two secret presses. From one, probably located at Lostock, the seat of the Andertons, issued a number of Catholic books." We are aware that other books were issued and that Lawrence Anderton wrote under the name of John Brierley is said to be the author of the well-known hymn *Jerusalem my happy home*. A heresy hunt was being vigorously pursued in the county and the printing press at Birchley was confiscated together with a number of books.

There is the story of Richard Mather, the Lowton boy, who was recommended from the Winwick Grammar School to become master of a Toxteth school and was later sent by an admiring people to university for clerical training. He was afterwards ordained by the Bishop of Chester who was greatly impressed by the sincerity of this young clergyman. Mather's increasing popularity served as an excuse for investigating the report "that he refused to comply with, or observe, the ceremonies of the Episcopal Church." A disciplinary committee sat at Wigan in 1634 and suspended him from preaching. In 1635 he emigrated to America and was received cordially at Dorchester. His youngest son was President of Harvard University for almost twenty years. Both sons and grandsons were exceptionally brilliant scholars. When inspecting land at Lowton, I turned to the occupier and said "Do you know where the house is in which Richard Mather was born?" pointing to a heap of bricks and rubble the man said "There are the remains of the house." Incredible! The Americans have set aside a building as a museum in which may be seen articles of furniture, cutlery, pottery, in fact anything which belonged to this notable family, while we have not even erected a plaque to perpetuate the memory of so famous a man. Four beautifully bound volumes of Mather's books were shown to me but the owner would not sell them, even for one hundred pounds.

We may follow a line to Byrom Hall, the property of the Byrom family. John Byrom is shown as holding land in Golborne, Lowton, Pennington, West Leigh, Warrington, Hindley, Abram and St. Helens in 1584. His son, Henry, was killed at the Battle of Edgehill. At five years of age he had been married to Margaret Bewsey of Warrington who was nine years of age. The marriage was celebrated at Bewsey, but was not consummated. Later in life, Margaret Bewsey married John Jefferies. George Jefferies, their son, well deserved the name by which he is best known: Bloody Jefferies.

Early in tne Civil War Thomas Jelland, writing from Atherton in December 1642, states that:

> *A battle between Derby's troops and the country*
> *people of Leigh and Lowton Common took place,*
> *several thousand troops of horse and men were*
> *encountered. About 200 horses and men were captured*
> *or killed. We never lost a man, only a few were wounded.*
> *The Naylers of Chowbent (Atherton)*
> *instead of making nayles have busied themselves making*
> *Bills and Battleaxes.*

Holcroft Hall, Culcheth was then occupied by Colonel Holcroft. He was M.P. for Wigan, 1645-48 , and keeper of the Peace for Golborne, Lowton, and Ashton. He was present at the siege of Winwick, and during the affray between the Royalists and Cromwell's troops he came in contact with one Thomas Blood. Blood visited Holcroft Hall and made the acquaintance of Maria Holcroft and eventually married her. It was this Thomas Blood who in Charles II's reign devised the notorious plot to steal the Crown Jewels from the tower. The story of his capture, sensational pardon, and the granting of a pension by the King reads more like fiction than fact. Blood was quite capable of brazen effrontery and, judging from the reports available, we presume that he exercised a kind of hypnotic spell over Charles II.

Colonel Thomas Blood left, who married Maria Holcroft of Holcroft Hall, pictured below, which is still standing.

Chapter XI
This is Your Parish, Beautify It

It is not enough to know that we have a heritage of beauty. However small, it is still ours to be regarded as a trust for posterity and as far as possible preserved. Although we cannot restore all the beauties of former days, we can cultivate a sense of admiration for all admirable things. Wordsworth, ever a true lover of nature, reminds us that "we live by admiration, hope and love," and to live truly we must see truly. Fortunately, there are a few people who have a sense of true values, though it is regrettable that the preservation of simple beauty is so often regarded as an extravagance unless it has a rateable value. It is the cynic who "knows the price of everything and the value of nothing." We have but little left to us of natural beauty; what remains is principally due to an Amenities Committee who had the foresight to schedule for preservation the woodland on the south side of the district stretching from Golborne Dale to Golborne Hollows. We hope that the woodland within Newton and Haydock, forming an additional adornment to the landscape, may be likewise preserved.

Bird Life

With the increase in population and the progress of industry there is less sanctuary for birds in and around Golborne. Some of the rarer specimens native to the district have almost disappeared. Cats and catapults, air-guns and shot-guns and the indiscriminate taking of birds eggs have affected our bird population. Many of the lovely coloured varieties such as blue tits, linnets and various finches which made the gardens their natural habitat are rarely seen. At one period along the quieter reaches of the Millingford, water coots, redshanks, snipe, wild duck and those uncommon and brilliantly coloured birds, the kingfishers, were to be seen. They have not completely left the district for at the time of writing few have been seen in the seclusion of Dean Dam and a pair of grey wild doves are nesting in the woods. Pheasants are becoming rarer, but the partridge family has not perceptibly lessened. During the days of returning spring and in the early summer nights the woods are filled with song. *Blithely sings the thrush*; the rich mellow cadences of the blackbird are heard, and occasionally the willow warbler sings in rapturous delight - a happy reminder of what might have been - had more serious consideration been given to these sweet singers of the woodlands.

Before the end of the last century, the secluded lands of Lightshaw served almost as a bird sanctuary. Large flocks of lapwings (pewits) gathered there, and during the nesting season plover eggs were plentiful. Epicureans regarded these as an attractive delicacy and were prepared to pay up to sixpence each for them. This was an inducement to the trespasser and poacher who took advantage of every favourable occasion to pilfer the eggs. The birds, which have a high reputation for keeping down insect life, are now much less plentiful. Reports have been recently received of herons, as many as twenty have been seen standing together in groups like silent sentinels in the shallow waters awaiting their prey.

Large flocks of starlings may often be seen. These useful birds are at present under suspicion, being blamed as carriers of the dreaded virus of Foot and Mouth disease. We are not prepared to regard them as pests until more reliable evidence is established. When spring-time cultivations of the land are in progress we have noticed how these birds have effectively acted as scavengers on wireworm infested ground. Regardless of the presence of men or machines they may be seen busily engaged in collecting and carrying off to their nesting quarters, thousands of the wireworm pests so destructive to various crops. But the true bird lover is making his influence felt. The embalmed specimens of birds mounted in glass cases happily have disappeared from most households. The living realities of beauty and song deserve and receive our protection.

In our lanes and hedgerows and above all in our woodland trees, we have many admirable specimens. It is unfortunately impracticable for each of us actually to plant a tree and in doing so help to make our world a more interesting and happy dwelling place for ourselves and those who succeed us, but we can safeguard this wonderful heritage by protecting newly planted roadside trees, and by treating with respect those monarchs which have been planted by nature and which in their rugged grandeur beautify our fields and woods. Visitors to the district have frequently remarked on the stately beauty of the trees. The many beech trees with towering height and rich luxuriant foliage make a superb ornament of beauty. Well may they with the great spread of their branches be called the mother of forests. The oak, although not attaining the perfection of the forest specimens, has a sturdy independence and vigour all its own. Man with his three score and ten years is ephemeral compared with these centuries old examples of durability. Ash, hazel, sycamore the *lady of the woods* - the graceful birch - we have all these and more. Here in the woods "is perpetual youth; here decorum and sanctity reign, a perennial festival is dressed, and the guest sees not how he should tire of them in a thousand years." (Emerson). From the early days of Spring to the declining days of Autumn the trees are a delight to eye and mind.

One of the pleasantest walks is along Sandy Lane better known as Keeper's or Carr's Lane, a name which doubtless originated with a former occupant of the lane's only cottage (White Doors Lodge). For some distance the roadway provides a boundary between Golborne and Haydock. From 1870 to 1880 it was principally an occupation way with hawthorn fences on both sides. With the returning days of early summer May blossom appeared in profusion. Convolvulus, briar roses and honeysuckle made a gorgeous festival of colour and perfume. The unenclosed woods were carpeted with bluebells. Then came the vandals. The place attracted trippers who came in vehicles of various kinds and made periodic forays on the flowers, even tearing up the honeysuckle by the roots. Now little of the former glory remains.

And so we say
And say it to their shame
That all was beauty here,
Until they came.

From the gateway of the White Doors Lodge is a carriageway leading to Haydock Lodge. This track runs for a distance under an avenue of trees, many of them Spanish chestnuts which, when in full flower, provide an attractive canopy. Human neglect has contributed remorselessly to its decay. Perhaps some future benefactor may allow this small enclosure to be used as one of the amenities of the township.

More rustic beauty is to be found in the banks of fern and bracken, in the profusion of wild flowers, stately trees and miniature lakes where water-fowl gather. These birds when suddenly surprised glide noiselessly away leaving a silvery streak in the water as they settle elsewhere among the rushes.

During 1925 a society known as The Men of the Trees was formed. Their object was: "To develop a tree sense in every citizen and to encourage all to plant, protect and love their native trees, for forestry is among the oldest and most honourable and peaceful arts of men, and its practice is unselfish and of constant service."

The Duke of Windsor, when Prince of Wales, sent several hundred beech saplings to Canada, and these were planted by The Men of the Trees Movement as an encouragement to Canada to attach even more importance to her forest trees. Surely, if a country so vast and rich in natural resources needs to be encouraged, are we not lacking in vision in allowing the beauty remaining to us to decline and disappear? Difficulties there may be, but if we can teach a younger generation to preserve, admire and develop a love for all such living specimens of beauty, the effort will not have been in vain. "To make men love their country" as Burke said, "We must make the country lovely. Beauty serves an enduring purpose that is an end in itself."

Chapter XII
1955-1975

During the last twenty years Golborne has seen many changes. With population increase and an extension of boundaries the township has grown considerably. Many new housing estates have been built and homes for Senior Citizens have been provided.

From a population of 1,657 in 1841 the population had increased to 7,322 in 1931. Two years later the addition of Lowton, Kenyon, part of Culcheth and other districts brought the population to an estimated 13,743. The estimate for 1972 was 28,630.

Civic pride has grown along with this development. A coat of arms with the motto *Fide et Fiducia* - by Faith and Confidence - was granted on 10th May, 1954 and a civic hall was opened in 1963. Changes in local government have taken place. The Urban District which had been established in 1894 was reorganised after the passing of the 1972 Local Government Act as a result, in 1974, Heath Park joined Abram, while St. Thomas, Lowton East and West became part of the Wigan Metropolitan District in the county of Greater Manchester. Culcheth and Newchurch wards were included in Warrington District, Cheshire. By 1973 the rateable value had increased to 2,482,045, the general rate being 37p in the pound.

Nationalisation - an especial feature of the years 1945-50 - affected Golborne along with the rest of the country. The North West Gas Company now supplies the gas, and, instead of the Lancashire Electric Power Company providing the electricity, the North West Electricity Board has this responsibility. Until 1964 the Ince Waterworks, situated in Golborne, supplied the water. Then the Makerfield Water Board with a Treatment Works on the same site took over. We are still supplied from there although now by the North West Region Water Authority.

Nationalisation and reorganisation of the railways brought the closing of Golborne station in 1960. Main roads, however, have been improved. The East Lancs Road constructed on the south side of the township in 1934 has been widened. It forms a link with the M6, one of the country's first motorways.

The coal mines, under state control since 1947, are still one of the town's main industries. Unfortunately, Naylors Engineering works soon after being sold to a larger concern has been closed down. The Parkside mills passed from Harbens to Courtaulds then to Tattons. They now produce such man-made fibres as terylene and crimplene. The industry flourishes as the export market expands.

One section of Harben's mill was taken over by the Imco Container Company. Since 1962 this member of an American combine has made plastic containers in Golborne. C.R. Harrison and Sons, Ltd., members of the Rank organisation, continue to produce seats for cinemas, theatres and lecture halls in Golborne as well as in Lowton where they took over the Sovereign Toffee buildings. Brookside mill when no longer used as a paper mill was occupied by H.S. Whiteside and Co. Ltd, during the war for the production of their *SunPat* products. Afterwards it stood empty for a while, then, after a fire, it was pulled down a few years ago. Mather's jam works continues and has built up an important export trade.

Important changes have taken place in education. After the 1944 Education act the council school became a Secondary Modern school. This became two schools in 1955 when the girls were transferred to a new building in Lowton Road. The two amalgamated in 1968 to form a Comprehensive school now attended by more than one thousand pupils.

In recent years a few more amenities have been provided for the town - a new library is the latest of these. Much could be done, however, to extend these, to beautify the town and to justify a pride in its history.

(This chapter was written in 1975 by Mary Bridge, daughter of the author, to mark the publication of *Gleanings of Golborne History*, which appeared 20 years after his death.)

Bibliography

Chapter I   Golborne's Past.
Victoria County History
History of the County of Lancashire   Baines
History and the Common Reader   Trevelyan
Ancient Crosses of Lancashire   Taylor
Ecclesiastical History or England   Bede
The Anglo-Saxon Chronicle
Anglo-Saxon Britain   Weigall
Local Gleanings   Worsley
Growth of the Manor   Vinogradoff
Constitutional History of England   Prosser & Sharp
Short History or England   Green

The Hundred
          The Hundred and Hundred Rolls   Cam
          West Derby Hundred   Eckwall

The Domesday Enquiry
          Domesday: Lancs.and Cheshire,V.C.H. Beamont

Terms Used in Domesday Book
          Law Lexicon   Wharton

The Newton Hundred in the Middle Ages
          Lancs, and Cheshire Inquisition   Rylands
          The Fee of Makerfield, Lancs,and   Beamont
          Cheshire Historical Society, Feb. 1872
          Bradshaws of Haigh   Hawkes
          The Hollands   Holland
          Coram Rage Roll 254   Tupling
          The Banastres
          Rambles Around Wigan   True
          Rambles Around Wigan   Bridgeman

Country Characters
    Travels in Lancashire   Young

Decline of the Craftsman
    Craftsmen All   Dryad Press

Chapter IV Industry
Cotton Manufacture
    Economic History of Europe   Clough & Cole
    History or Derbyshire
    Leigh Chronicle   Rose
    Leigh in the Eighteenth Century   Rose

Wallpaper Manufacture
    Local History   Newton

The Golborne Gas Company
    Parish Council Minutes, 1883

Chapter V Transport - Roads
    The King's Highway   Webb
    Golborne Parish Council Minutes
    Leland"s Itinerary 1533-1559   Smith
    The Pastons and their England   Bennett
    1770 Travels   Young
    Green Roads Of England   Cox
    The Journeys of Celia Fiennes   ed. Morris
    The Old Straight Track   Watkin
    Law of Highway   Pratte

Railways
    Local History   Lane

Chapter VI The Church
Lowton Chapel Agreement
Lancashire Church Survey

Church Commission

Dora Greenwell: Devotional Writer
Wm. Dorling Memoirs
Life of Dora Greenwell
Miss Manyard   Bett
Canon Greenwell's Discoveries

Chapter VII
Law and Order
    Ecclestiastical Courts
    Tudor Constitutional Documents   Tanner
    England Under the Stuarts   Ogg
    History or Winwick   Beamont

Chapter VIII
Sports and Pastimes
    Games and Gamesters   Cotton
    Its My Delight   Fitzgerald
    Lives of the Gamesters, 1714   Lucas
    Cockfighting: Newton History   Lane

Customs
    History of England   Macaulay
    Lancashire & Cheshire Wills Vol.37
    Historical Society
    Folk Lore   Gould
    Lancashire Customs   Taylor

Superstitions
    Lancashire Sayings   Taylor
    These Charming Acres   Noden

Chapter IX
Local Sayings & Writings-Dialect
    Glossary   Nodal & Milner
    Local Gleanings - Lancs & Cheshire   Earwaker
    Leigh Chronicle   Rose
    Diary of Roger Lowe   Sasche